Learn
Apply
&
Grow
Rich

Learn
Apply
&
Grow
Rich

It is about you, your family and your legacy!

ROLAND G. STEWART

For more information, please visit https://www.vpfranchises.com/.

ISBN: 979-8-88759-278-7 (paperback)
ISBN: 979-8-88759-279-4 (ebook)

Cover designed by Jeanly Zamora

Printed in the U.S.A.

This book is dedicated to…

Everyone who believed in us and encouraged us. Thank you. Thank you very much.

Thanks so much for purchasing *Learn Apply and Grow Rich!* I would like to show my appreciation to you by offering you a free gift, available at continueforward@live.com.

Visit <u>continueforward@live.com</u> to claim yours today!

Here's to your RICH future!

Gib

CONTENTS

INTRODUCTION

Be RICH
We Didn't Want to be Poor

This book tells the story of a couple, my wife and I. When the two of us were confronted with situation after situation, we decided to do something other than just accept the status quo. We decided time and time again to deal with each situation in a way that worked for us, no matter how much it upset the community's norms.

The short story is that we started with a net worth of two hundred and eighty-eight dollars. In the ensuing sixteen years, we accumulated just over $2 million dollars net, and in the following eighteen years, we built our family estate and it is still growing. We now manage well over $70 million dollars' worth of property for ourselves and our co-owners. We did it all one step at a time, slowly learning as we tried to move forward continually. We believed. We learned. We applied. We thrived, and then, all of a sudden, we were RICH.

Suggestion from the Editor

I suggest that while you read this book, you take notes or use a pen, pencil, or highlighter to mark up the book. I believe there is a lot to be learned here.

Learn, Apply, *and* **Grow Rich!**

1. **Learn the principles:** When finished with this book, you'll understand the concepts of *how* to grow rich.
2. **Apply the principles**: Apply and *continue* forward!
3. **Grow RICH**: Each day is an opportunity to grow rich in whatever way *you* have decided to grow RICH. That could be financially, religiously, in relationships, or even politically. Believe!

Here is some of what I hope you learn while reading this book:

Know yourself—what can you do,
What are you willing to do?
Know who you are working with at all times.
Does the person you are working with have
the stamina and direction you have?
Walk away from "downers" and "nay-sayers."
Associate with the five "best" people possible.
What is your "Why"?
What is your partner's "Why"?
Can they co-exist?
What is your goal?
What is your plan? (It will change or at
least modify as you progress.)
Learn basic math.
Read.
Continue to learn.

Be ready when an offer/opportunity presents itself.
Take advantage of opportunities.
Do not self-eliminate.
Know your marketplace.
Take calculated risks.
Measure your growth at least annually.
The first $10,000 is the hardest.
Focus.
Decide to decide.
Learn from failure.
Focus on successes.
Have a mantra.
Persist.

Thanks for reading,

Gib

I believe, I know that you are able and so now
you need to believe and continue forward!

SECTION 1

How to Get Started?

Something has to work.

CHAPTER 1

Where It All Started for Us

This story must start here:

I stood in a parking lot in Hopkinsville, Kentucky. The day was sunny and comfortable—no humidity that day. It was late July 1970, and it was nice that the humidity had lifted. Cool and comfortable. I was just enjoying the absolutely beautiful weather when up drove a beautiful young girl, and she said to me, "Shall we go get some ice cream?"

That's my story, but, of course, there is more to it, and her story is slightly different. First of all, it was a church parking lot. And then there is the rest of the story.

The Backstory

I should take a giant step back at this point since neither of us just came to be that July day in 1970. Here is some of my earlier story.

I was raised Catholic-military. That means that my family attended Catholic Church. My parents were very devout. We, the five of us, went to church every Sunday, and I mean *every* Sunday. I had an older sister, Madeline, who was everything to me, and a younger brother, George. My father sold medical supplies to support the family, but his main focus, his happiness, was being an Army reservist. He had served in WWII and chose to stay in the reserves after the war. The two careers worked for him. As my father moved to better and better medical equipment companies and better territories, he could change from one military unit to another and grow both arenas at the same time. He retired as Lieutenant Colonel Roland L. Gibson.

I was born in south Seattle, Washington, and grew up in Gresham, Oregon, and Los Altos, California. And I graduated from Morningside High School in Inglewood, CA. I had attended four high schools along the way. I attended and graduated from Linfield College in McMinnville, Oregon. I washed out of basketball my junior year, switched to track, and helped set an NAIA regional record in the 4x110 relay. Linfield graciously allowed me to graduate in 1969 with one of the lowest grade point averages in school history. After graduation, I started hitch-hiking around the country, and a few weeks into that, my draft notice (allegedly) arrived in SoCal. I turned immediately and signed up in the United States Army with the option to go to Officer Candidate School. Throughout my "military career," I had a guardian angel on my shoulder.

Return to the Vignette ...

My roommate, a fellow second lieutenant, Darryl Houck, and I lived in a rental house adjacent to the church parking lot. One very balmy Saturday afternoon, Darryl and I were sitting in the living room watching television as a contingent of bugs, of various shapes and sizes but in a straight line, sauntered across the wooden living room floor between us and the television.

Time for us to move. *Not putting up with this any longer.*

This all took place in Hopkinsville, Kentucky, a small town a few miles from Fort Campbell. Darryl and I were single, recent college graduates, and newly-minted Second Lieutenants, OCS Fort Sill, Oklahoma, class 13-69, destined for an uncharted future with the exception that we would most likely end up as forward observers for some infantry platoon in Viet Nam.

I'd been a regular at the church, a Catholic Church, for several weeks. After all, I had been brought up Catholic-military, so I was just doing what I was supposed to do. Having grown up Catholic, I had a feel for how helpful a local priest could be, so the next Saturday, I marched over to the church rectory adjacent to the parking lot and knocked on the rectory door. Father Italy, a former military chaplain, and a really nice, likable guy, answered the door. I said, "Father, do you know anyone who would rent a reasonable place to a couple of soldiers? I'm not very fond of all of these "no dogs, no soldiers allowed" signs, and my roommate and I are not comfortable where we are."

So, we discussed housing options, and he gave me some ideas and some names and phone numbers that might be helpful. Then, I said, "Thank you," and started to leave.

Then, out of the blue, Father Italy asked me, "Do you have anything else on your mind?" We discussed the possibility of my coaching the grade school basketball team. I had played ball from age 12, was a starter on a team that won a state championship, had lettered in college, and loved the sport. We talked about it, and he told me that even being a grade school coach in Kentucky was very much a political position, and I wouldn't get the job, and if I did happen to get the job, it would be a horrible experience.

Father Italy persisted, "Do you have anything else you need?"

Well, then I told him, "I'd sure like to meet some reasonable girls as I have just moved to the area and have not met any." Once that was on the table, he told me about and gave me the phone number of the girl who picked me up in the parking lot.

As it turned out, Bobby Rich, an OCS classmate, was renting from the local high school secretary. Because of Bobby's connection, I was able to do quite a bit of research about "the girl" before I called her. She had been runner-up for homecoming queen, class secretary her senior year, and she ran sprints for the track team. That all sounded good to me and the photos looked good too. I loved that she ran sprints, as I ran sprints for many years. Also, I believed in the value of holding a class office. I had even been class president in college. Needless to say, it all sounded like it was worth at least a phone call.

When I called her, Grace was more than reluctant to meet me. Once I explained that Father Italy had given me her name, she, still quite reluctantly, agreed to meet me. At that point, I asked how to get to her place, and she told me it was much too complicated, country back roads and all, so we agreed to meet in the church parking lot.

Marriage, the Army, and Traveling

Grace Blewett and I were married on December 15, 1970. Grace's parents were well-known farmers in the area, but they did live quite a ways "out of town." Grace's family was fun. She had seven siblings, so the family was always doing something—lots of family and lots and lots of fun.

The first couple of years of married life were easy, full of fun, with some minor accomplishments.

6

The fun and adventure included travel to places like Kansas, Ohio, Texas, Tennessee, and other states. It also included free professional basketball games and the Kentucky Derby.

Once, when I got in trouble at work, I was assigned the duty of escorting enlisted personnel to a dance in Hopkinsville. I reported to the special services officer and made arrangements. The day came for the dance, and I showed up as ordered. However, no one wanted to go to the dance. As a consolation prize, the special services officer, knowing I had played basketball in college, offered me the commanding general's tickets to the Kentucky Colonels ABA basketball games whenever the general didn't want to use them. Due to my getting in trouble, Grace and I attended a number of games that year.

Accomplishments during this time period included Grace's starring in the stage production of *Denny and the Witches*. **Hint:** She was not one of the witches. Her graduation from community college was a big step forward for us as a couple. Once she graduated, her continuing education was always a part of our planning. We wanted her to get a degree and an education.

During this time, I was fortunate enough to become a company commander of a basic training unit. Eventually, a few months after Grace's graduation, I lost that job because a captain reported for duty and therefore was "more qualified" for the job. I then became an assistant in the plans and training headquarters unit. I learned then that I didn't like a job where I had to ride a desk.

Eventually, my orders for Viet Nam came. Based on a rumor, and at Darryl's suggestion, I requested to go through a field artillery refresher course. After being accepted to the refresher course, Grace and I moved to Oklahoma, so I could take the course at Fort Sill.

CHAPTER 2

Army Life Part 2

After checking in for my refresher class, Grace and I found a nice apartment in Lawton. It was over a garage. We paid something like $73 a month, much less than my military housing allowance, so we felt we were "making money." Grace tried to go to college, but we found out that we would have to pay out-of-state tuition. She tried to find a job. Again no luck. Then we found out about a free craft shop on post, so she took classes at the craft shop and started making crafts we hoped to be able to sell.

My orders for Viet Nam were still in place after graduating from the refresher class. I went into a holdover unit awaiting "the date." About three days before I was to fly out of Travis Air Force Base, I went into my headquarters unit to sign out and head to Travis and from there on to Viet Nam. Our plan was for Grace to drive down to Laguna Woods, CA, and hopefully either work toward her degree or get a job while I was overseas.

When I walked into headquarters, I was greeted nicely and handed the sign-out log. As I looked through the log to see who had signed out recently, a sergeant came out from behind a desk and asked if I was Lieutenant Gibson.

I said I was, and he said, "Sir, the Pentagon called for you this morning; please call this major back." He handed me a paper with a name and phone number on it. I told the NCO that he probably pulled this prank on everyone signing out for Nam, and although it was funny, I didn't think I would call the number.

With some encouragement from him, I called, and the major who answered the phone asked me, "Do you still want to go to Viet Nam?"

I said, "Why do you ask?" I don't know what inspired me to ask that question; it was not a question I was used to asking. I grew up in a family where you didn't ask questions; you did what you were told.

At any rate, the major explained that President Nixon had just given every officer a two-month drop-in time remaining in service and that my two-month drop put me down to five months and twenty-eight days. Therefore, it was illegal (in those days) for the military to send me to a combat zone without my permission. I had less than six months left in the service unless I requested to go.

I explained that I had just married, so I preferred not to go.

I was then told to go find myself a job. I did not want the responsibility of being a range officer (verifying where artillery rounds might land), so my first call was to Special Services to see if they could use an officer. I ended up being Assistant Residential Security Officer for Fort Sill, Oklahoma. A great way to spend my last one hundred seventy-seven days in the service.

And so Grace and I started making arts and crafts together at the fort's craft center. It was to be our first business venture.

A failure, but, like most of our failures, it was fun trying, and we learned a great deal.

Europe

With the end of the army years in sight, Grace and I began to talk about what we should do after I signed out. Talk quickly turned to travel. (When we met, Grace had only been in two states in her life: Kentucky and Indiana.) Since our marriage, she had been in large parts of more than ten states. We both enjoyed traveling. Eventually, we decided to take an "'as long as we can" trip to Europe. So, when I was released, we drove to Laguna Woods, CA, and worked toward finalizing our plan.

Once at my folk's house, we took a couple of days at Disneyland as our honeymoon, and then I started seeking information. A week or so later, we were on a plane to London.

We spent 88 days in Europe, North Africa, and Asia—an unbelievable experience.

Can't Buy a Job

President Richard Nixon let me out of the army two months early. We may have "wasted" almost three months in Europe, but we had plans. After returning to the USA, we made a short stop in Laguna Woods, then headed north to get Grace back in school. We were headed to Eugene, Oregon, and the University of Oregon. When we reached Eugene, I started looking for a job. Lots of guys were looking for a job. Many had just been released from the military. The economy wasn't doing that well, and times were tough.

Grace and I tried selling some of our craft work, but we didn't get that business started. Eventually, I was hired in Corvallis, Oregon. I had to commute 45 to 55 minutes each way, every day. After a few months, my boss at Beneficial Finance put me up for a fast-track program. I was accepted, and the company moved us to Oakland, California. Grace finished out a second term at the University of Oregon, then joined me in Oakland. Her education was our priority. If something happened to me and she had her degree, she could support herself. This meant we needed to carry less life insurance on me. A double win, financially.

No one on the West Coast had ever been able to finish Beneficial Finance Corporation's EOST *(Educate Operations Special Trainers* program). With that as a bit of knowledge, I figured I had a pretty good chance of getting some good support. The West Coast division had to catch up with the other divisions. It didn't work out like that; however, I did make it through the program but at a horrible price. Stupid.

As it turned out, my first boss was dating my coworker and contemporary. They would leave the store on the button at 5:00 and leave me to finish the day's work.

When she arrived, Grace quickly found work as a retail sales clerk at Rhodes department store. She soon realized she did not like being a retail clerk, so she started looking for a different job. Meanwhile, I continued to work a great deal of overtime. I was not smart enough to figure out a different way. Sad.

CHAPTER 3

A Start toward Our Investment Dream

Our investment history begins in this atmosphere in late 1974. We were living in Oakland, CA. Grace had moved to a temporary position as a ten-key operator for Texaco, and I was still a management trainee for Beneficial Finance, making loans. Grace had actually been Texaco's second choice. The person who received the job quit after one day. Over the years, Grace and I would discover that in business, as opposed to sports, second place can be a really good place to be.

Grace, who brought a positive net worth of $525 to our family, had taught me how to save. I had brought a negative net worth of $237 to the family, so we started with a family net worth of $288. Why did I figure that out? I do not know. That was all we had "in the beginning." She had a free and clear automobile and some savings, and I had some cash but a lot of debt: a new powder-green Mustang, a new stereo set, and a new television set. Neither of our families had any money, but for very different reasons. She was from a farm family, and I was from an upwardly mobile, spend-what-you-have big city family.

Even though Grace and I had spent the previous years, our army years, as a one, small income family, we had managed to save a few thousand dollars. A few thousand dollars was a lot of money in those days. Our average savings, except during our trip to Europe, had been almost 70 percent of our net income each month during the years one or more of us had been working. Now that we both had jobs, we decided to live on the smaller income and save the larger income. This was a big decision, and it served us well. We weren't making much money working and so we both knew that we'd never be as financially comfortable as we wanted to be unless we figured out a way to get an outside income. We decided to invest.

Grace was raised on a farm and had always lived with the fear that "the crop might not come in," so we decided that our game plan, our method of budgeting, would be that every time we did a budget, we would maximize spending estimates (debt) and minimize income estimates with the goal being to live on the lower income and to save everything that was left at the end of the month.

Minimizing income meant, to us, living on one income, the lower income. Travel is cheap when you have a tent and two sleeping bags. Exercise is easy and a great time to catch up when you both really enjoy walking. Life is pretty inexpensive if neither of you likes to drink or smoke. And neither of us wanted the responsibility, maintenance, or expense of a pet. We were just a couple of nerds, and we were doing well.

We saved a lot every month, never knowing what the next month might bring. It was fun for us as we just needed to be creative and not do what other people wanted us to do. My parents were our biggest critics. That was tough, but it helped make me become more of an individual.

We had goals. We had fun figuring out how to track money and finding new ways to do almost everything. Interesting times. Fun times.

The First Investment

Once we thought we had enough to start investing, we took our money to Merrill Lynch, met a very experienced stock broker who taught us a great deal, and we started investing. With his help and guidance, we used his technique for a couple of years, and our nest egg grew and grew. Then, out of the blue, one day, we received a call and found out that we had a new stock broker. We were told that the first stock broker had received a job managing a large segment of Stanford University's foundation's funds. Great for him, not so great for us. As it turns out, our next three investments, based on the advice of our new stock broker, were all busts, and we lost all of our investments, all of our investment money. Every. Single. Penny.

It was time for us to leave the stock market; the broker hadn't salvaged a single penny, and so we were going to need to started over. We were going to need to double down on saving. Not that we had ever stopped, but we were starting all over again from an investment standpoint. We decided we didn't have any control over the stock market. We were working too hard for our money to play that lottery system.

About this time, I figured out why I was willing to save and invest. There must be a compelling "why." We knew Grace's reason, and that was: the crops might not come in. My "why" turned out to be that I did not like working and did not want to be poor. Now I realize it isn't that I don't like working because I do. It is more that I don't like working for someone else.

Early on, I had a basic belief in the stock market. Shortly after Grace and I married, I wrote to ten of my good friends from college in an attempt to start an investment group, a mutual fund. None of the guys ever wrote back—not one. I suspect that none of them had accumulated the $1,000 initial investment needed to start the fund.

All in all, considering what had just happened to our nest egg, I am glad we didn't get into the mutual fund business, and I am really very glad that I didn't get any of the guys interested in starting a mutual fund. If we had failed, I would not have known how to recover, let alone pay all of them back for their investment with me.

Take Off and Burn Out

Grace's job had become permanent, and she'd received a raise or two or three. The fact is she was taken on full-time and permanently. And then, she was assigned an actual desk instead of being a floater covering for vacations and sick leave. The work assigned to the desk didn't make sense to her, so she asked a supervisor to explain the workings to her. Eventually, everyone decided that Texaco had been double paying a very significant bill rather than receiving a refund of the same size. Grace rightfully got the credit for saving Texaco hundreds of thousands of dollars or probably a whole lot more based on our estimates as we learned more about the numbers involved.

I was starting to make some reasonable money too. I was up the ladder a little at Beneficial, having just been appointed to run my first office. I was up the ladder but working so much that for a couple of months that year, I didn't even see the sun, except on a Sunday here and there. Eventually, after twenty-one months or so, my workload and the strain of feeling that I had to, that I must succeed, led to disaster. My body shut down. I could not walk and talk at the same time. I could still talk and laugh, but nothing, almost nothing more—time to punt.

Now What?

Just weeks before my shutdown, I had been contacted by a friend from high school and college. The friend, Len, had once been written up in Time and Newsweek as one of the "new brand of young millionaires." I think Len is the reason I was accepted into a reasonable university. Len thought I was a good athlete and, I think, told the university they should talk to me.

At any rate, Len had decided to start an investment newspaper and wanted me to work for him again. I had worked for him for a while during high school and again during college, and he thought I could guide his sales team. The job opportunity gave me an out. It would also give me less stress and time to recover, so, I gave notice and I moved to Tacoma, Washington. Within days I was working with Len. Grace followed.

CHAPTER 4

A College Degree

Grace had been so valuable to and such a good worker for Texaco that when she went into the office to explain that we had decided to move to Tacoma, they offered her a transfer to their south Seattle office. She took the transfer, and Texaco created a job for her in the steno pool.

My job at the newspaper paid our base living expenses (next to nothing), but it did allow us to continue saving Grace's salary. A year later, after we earned residency, Grace was able to go back to school to finish her degree. She'd completed her first two years in the community college system in Kentucky. She'd also finished two quarters of college while working as a student at the University of Oregon. Texaco again did well by Grace. Texaco allowed her to keep her job and work during school breaks. It took her four quarters to earn her degree, and then she was hired full-time at Texaco as one of the first female sales reps for Texaco USA.

Grace began selling tires, batteries, and accessories to Texaco dealers. Initially, she turned down the job and thought she might like to work for another type of business. It didn't take her long or many interviews to figure out that her new job at Texaco would pay her a whole lot more money than any other employer.

During the same period, the newspaper failed, and I started trying job after job to find something interesting and enjoyable that I could actually do. I was still very "messed up." The doctor I was seeing said that my Valgus nerve had shut down. I was seeking a job where I could thrive; instead, I kept landing in positions that left me either feeling unsuccessful or not enjoying the work.

Eventually, my mind and body started functioning again. It took years. To this day, I still suffer some intermittent, short-term shutdowns. I hate it, but it is what it is, telling me to sleep, get some rest and move away from the "flame," whatever the "flame" might be.

The recovery wasn't quick. It was long, long time before it started, almost a year, and then very, excruciatingly gradual until I could function reasonably well. Because we didn't know if I would ever recover, it was a very scary time for us. It must have been quite a concern for Grace. She encouraged me, but she never complained. It was a very rough time in our life, in my life. One that I do not like to dwell on. If Grace had been most women, she would have left me.

A Chance Meeting

While recovering, I swam every day during the spring, summer, and early fall. I used the pool at the apartment complex where we lived. The only other person to use the pool at all regularly was Lou Cotton. Lou was living in the apartments because he was taking science classes at U of W in hopes of qualifying for dental school. We had some very good times and formed a long-term friendship. He was going to have a huge impact on Grace's and my lives and our investment future.

Try, Try, and Try AGAIN

About this time, I worked as a Fuller Brush sales person. For those of you too young to know, Fuller Brush was a residential door-to-door, person-to-person sales system. I decided to try to develop a route, a business. Something. Crazy. Who hadn't heard of two-income families? Obviously, I had no idea what was happening around me or what I was doing. I was just trying.

Fuller Brush, a company with a great reputation, also sent me some junk products. They were actually changing their business model right under my nose; I didn't notice. Alas, I failed pretty quickly. Next, we tried Tupperware. In those days, Tupperware was sold in a party setting. Gather acquaintances, have a party, and sell Tupperware. This was tough on Grace. Grace didn't mind selling via phone. She did not like standing in front of a group while trying to sell Tupperware. That went by the wayside pretty quickly too.

Then I tried working as a manufacturer's rep, selling pots, pans, and watches. I couldn't get the hang of that either. I felt like and was a failure. My boss and his right-hand person in Portland seemed to be making great money, and the opportunity for me was there. But I could not perform. I made a couple of other attempts to be productive and tried to make a living. Nothing seemed to work. Grace was thriving; I was down and out and a drain. For some reason, quite possibly our mutual Catholic upbringing, we stayed together.

Eventually, I ended up with a job as a body broker, selling bodies and jobs. This wasn't as gruesome as it sounds. I worked to develop jobs and then find the right people to fill them. It was very enjoyable work. I have always enjoyed helping people find work. I was good at interviewing and being interviewed. I seemed to be doing a good job of teaching people how to interview. But I couldn't make reasonable money. Another failure in the works, except I enjoyed the work and was getting people hired. Three of the guys I interviewed and found jobs for actually ended up being long-term friends.

Alas, how can I make money doing this type of work or something similar? I found one employer some great interviewees and at least one good employee. At one point, the employer and I had a couple of short chats about the idea of my doing human resource work for him. Then he walked away from the idea. I then thought for a while about looking for that type of work, but then I realized, too much paperwork and desk time, and that was the end of that idea.

Buying a Home, November 1975

Grace was making what we thought was a tremendous amount of money. Furthermore, we thought I might now have half a chance of working a regular job. Maybe, since I was enjoying my work, I could find a job where I could eventually earn a reasonable living by doing it or something similar. I was 28 and still pretty much less than fully able, but it seemed I was "recovering." It was now 1975, and we began thinking of buying a house.

With inflation ramped up and with no end in sight, we started looking. We looked at more and more expensive houses. We looked and looked and looked. Ever a maker of useful lists, Grace had a list of some eighteen things she wanted in a house.

Eventually, we found a house that met fifteen of the eighteen "needs." Expensive? Yes, it was, but I was sure we could make the payments. We knew our lifestyle. We knew how to save. With a little skullduggery on my part, we ended up purchasing the house. I know that how we got the house then is now illegal, but that is due to recent changes in banking rules. Grace wanted the house, so I got it. That was my single criterion; Grace wanted it. Our new neighbors were all doctors, lawyers, university professors, and small business owners, and I was a pots and pans salesman, and not a very good one at that. And here we were, just two young kids among mature adults with kids, and we knew little of how to take care of a house or a yard.

Our loan was from the Department of Veterans Affairs. It was a great, low-interest loan. We were so very fortunate. It took a while because my military papers, my DD214, had been filled out incorrectly. The records are still wrong because when I enlisted, I had been asked, "Where do you want the Army to send your body?"

I gave them my parent's address in California. If I had been asked, "Where do you live?" Then they would have had the address of the McMinnville, Oregon, apartment complex where I lived. Unbelievably, I was able to find the senior NCO who was the manager of the Army recruiting office when I enlisted. I ran into him while shopping in a local grocery store one evening. Everyone involved in the loan process made things work. Once again, we were very fortunate.

CHAPTER 5

Some Permanence

With all these failed attempts to find a job, Grace and I knew something was wrong with me. I would often enjoy a new job, but within six to nine months, I'd be bored and eventually just tire of the job, or I wasn't even able to do it, or, let me face it, I just failed. Not good. A short while later, I decided to go to the employment security office in downtown Seattle. I went there because I had heard during my "back to civilian life" lecture when I was leaving the army that they would give free testing to veterans. They were trying to help us veterans find work, find a life.

The testing showed that I was in the right type of work. Working with people and helping them find work was the type of work I should do. But, the question for me was, "How can I make money doing this type of work?" Once I told the test administrator, Mrs. Hamer, that I agreed with the test results but that I couldn't make any money in that type of work, she went to work to help me.

Shortly after, I was working in an entry-level position with the State of Washington, helping people find jobs. My position was part-time and temporary but extremely enjoyable. No pressure. I was making something like $425 per month, extremely low wages for the times. Whatever, it had the potential to get better. I felt it could be permanent if only I could get a permanent position. The team I was working with was setting statewide records placing the most job applicants in a succession of months. Soon, someone from another team left, and I was able to get the job and be full-time—lots of fun. My new boss and I implemented a number of new systems to our team that made job placement even more productive. A short while later, I was actually a permanent employee—just in time. A new start.

The Next Step

Grace and I now both had permanent jobs, so we could try investing again. It was 1977, and inflation was still running rampant. We glanced ahead to make sure we could cover our tax bill. We found, to our concern, that we would owe $10,000 in taxes by the end of the year. Looking back, I'm not quite sure what happened, but it had something to do with Grace's job, her bonus, and my meager income all combined that really pushed the amount of tax we would need to pay. Probably something to do with not having enough taxes taken out of her bonuses.

We looked at our investment options. Grace asked what we could do to reduce our tax liability. I think I remember the statement, "I'm not working this hard to give my money to the government to spend," but I could be wrong. We decided to try real estate. We felt real estate would give us more control than we felt we had in the stock market. We also calculated that if we did real estate "properly," we probably would not have to pay that $10,000 in taxes. Our significant thoughts and ideas were that it would be better to risk losing the $10,000 than just handing it over to the government. So we started looking.

After many nights and weekends of analysis and searching, we purchased a small apartment complex. We had decided that a duplex was less expensive per unit than a house, and a triplex was less expensive per unit than a duplex, so we started watching and looking at all kinds of small apartment complexes. We ended up with a 14-unit complex, with 10 one-bedroom units, 2 two-bedroom units, and 2 three-bedroom units. We were starting.

How did we do it? We took out a second mortgage on our house and borrowed various amounts of money from five people who trusted us. The complex cost right around $250,000. That is a quarter of a million dollars—more than we could ever expect to save. And, we felt the prices would keep going up if inflation continued. That would give us all kinds of protection, and it gave us a retirement plan.

We had a real down payment! It was a new beginning. We had a chance again. If we didn't do anything additional by the time we retired, we would have a pretty significant personal retirement plan. All we needed to do was hang on.

SECTION 2

Grow, Grow, Grow

Seizing "Targets of Opportunity"

CHAPTER 6

A Chance

I would not borrow money or even talk about money with my father. Earlier, after I got out of the army and before Grace and I had any responsibilities, Grace and I decided we should see Europe. I had received a boatload of cash when I left the Army. I believe it might have been unused vacation pay. I made about a hundred telephone calls to find a cheap flight to Europe, and we were ready to leave. Just before we left, my father decided that we didn't have enough cash, so he really pushed on me to take out a loan, "Just in case."

I did and made arrangements with one of the bankers to deposit my payment check each month. One month the banker forgot to deposit the payment check, so my folks received notice. My dad had cosigned for me. My father had a real problem with the notice that the loan was going to be called, and he would be on the hook for the balance, or perhaps his credit was a little tenuous. Growing up, I had always feared that we would run out of money.

At any rate, a month later, when Grace and I returned from our trip, I went into the branch to find out what had happened. The banker was on some outside job. The banker at the next desk asked why I wanted to talk with the missing banker, and I explained. The banker at the next desk turned and told me that she knew what had happened; the payment hadn't been made on time because the banker who was supposed to help me had forgotten to make the payment. This was the first time I learned not to trust bankers, but it wasn't the last. And, after that disaster, I wouldn't ever discuss money with either of my parents ever again.

Grace's parents still had a number of young children at home, so that option was out too.

Five People Who Trusted Us

What an interesting world we had entered. I still have a very difficult time thinking that five people trusted us with their money. People just gave us loans anywhere from $2,500 to $5,000. That may not sound like a lot of money today, but in 1977 that was a lot of money. Compared to current times, $3,500 in 1977 is equal to $16,882 in 2022; and $250,000 is $1,205.842.

Here are *some* of the people who gave us our start:

- One of Grace's sisters, who had been saving up for college, loaned us $2,500.
- The mother of a deceased friend loaned us $3,500.
- My old boss at Beneficial gave me a $5,000 company loan.
- An entrepreneurial friend loaned us $3,500.

I don't know how Grace and I earned so much trust, but the money those people loaned us helped us "make it happen."

Nana Geneva

Our Nana, Geneva Pace, had raised two boys on her own, one of whom had been one of my best friends in college. He had died in an auto accident shortly after the two of us graduated from college. When Geneva met Grace, Geneva basically adopted us as a couple. Eventually, she, for all practical purposes, "adopted" each of our kids, not formally, but we felt that way. Nana's second son, whom I became friends with when we were working together to bury his brother, also died in an accident. Geneva also died in a tragic accident; a drunk driver ran over her while she was in a crosswalk, crossing a minor street. All were tough times for us, but all of that was in the years to follow. Geneva loaned us $3,500. *Wow*. I was grateful for the money but even more grateful that she adopted our family. She was a wonderful woman.

Sue Blewett

Sue Blewett, our young college student, Grace's sister/my sister-in-law, was another of our first backers. She knew how to save money almost as well as her older sister. She had lived with us for a number of months and was saving for college. It was nice of her to trust us with her savings; $2,500.

A side note here. Early in our marriage, Grace and I decided that we, like her oldest sister, Shirley, should try to help and encourage Grace's younger siblings. Shirley had encouraged Grace to get a degree. Grace had graduated and that was making a significant difference in our life. It was time for us to 'pay it forward'. To that end, each time one of Grace's siblings graduated from high school, we would have the new graduate come out and live with us for the summer wherever we lived. That would allow them to see a wider world. At this point in time, Sue was the most recent to stay with us, and, as it turned out, she was the only one who never went back to Kentucky.

R.V. Bealson

R. V. (Ron) Bealson, my former boss at Beneficial, was working for a loan company in Washington State, and he gave me a company loan of five thousand dollars, the most allowable by his new company. It was the first loan we paid back, as it was the only loan with an interest rate tied to it.

Byron Mo

An entrepreneurial friend, Byron Mo, lent us $3,500. I had met Byron when I was a body broker before I joined state government. Many years later, Byron called and told me he, too, had reached millionaire status. It is so nice to see nice people successful, especially long-term friends.

The Final Pieces, we thought

My college roommate, Mike Hinkle, bought into the venture for some $7,000.

Just before closing, I went to a friend from college who had become a real estate attorney. We sat in his living room, and he went through the 42-page financing document the seller had given me. Now, I know that document is usually referred to as a "Seller's Contract." I could only buy with seller financing as Grace and I didn't have any real credit background, and definitely, no real estate experience, and I did not have much of a job. Dale Hermanson looked through the document. He changed just three words in the document. *Three.* And, he charged us only like $75.00, which I was sure was a terrific deal. More on those three words later; they turned out to be incredibly important words for Grace and me.

Rude Awakening

Shortly after closing the deal, we found our first challenge. I received a call from the office manager of the builder who was carrying the contract. I guess we hadn't read the documentation quite well enough. They wanted their first payment.

HELP. We didn't have another $2,390 to our name, and we could not think of anywhere or any way to find it.

So, the only thing I could do was tell the truth. I took the city bus over to the builder's office and met with Chuck Lewiston, the builder's chief partner. We talked. I explained to Chuck that every cent I had and more was already spent to get into the building. Chuck suggested that we should "just add the payment to the back end of the contract." Yet another party loaned us 2,390 dollars . *Wow. Time to get the job done.*

After Chuck resolved my issue he told me that as long as we stayed in the residential real estate business we would have two significant issues. He said we would always have issues with parking and with keys. To this day both have been and are truly headaches.

CHAPTER 7

The First Move-Outs

Our first move-out. We received notice. *Great. Time to run an ad.* Time to prep for the turnover. And then, I saw the interior of the unit. It was one of the two units we couldn't access during our pre-purchase inspection, and it was going to be what I eventually labeled a "rake out." I literally had to take a garden rake and rake all the bits and pieces of paper out of the carpet before I could get the vacuum in to vacuum the carpet. If I hadn't raked the carpet, the vacuum would have burnt out its motor very quickly—what a way to start.

The second move-out was a midnight walk-out, a midnight move. Well, it wasn't really midnight. I had dropped Grace at school, where she was taking a course toward a master's degree, then I dropped by the apartment complex to work while she was in class, planning that I'd pick her up when class was finished. Well, I parked and walked into the courtyard to find all the furniture from one of the units sitting in the courtyard. I asked the tenant, "What's happening?"

She said simply, "I'm moving."

Now, what do I do?

Since Grace was in a "business law" class and the instructor had said something like, "ask me in class, and the answer is free, come to my office, and I will charge you." So, I quickly drove to town, found a parking place, ran to her classroom, and waved Grace out of class. She was reluctant, very reluctant at best, to walk out of class to talk with me. When she finally came to the door, I explained the issue. During break, she asked the instructor what I could do.

Could I throw the tenant down the stairs? Such is hardly my style, but I was somewhat desperate. If not, what other options did I have? The instructor told her, "He can help her load the truck if he wants, but nothing more."

Now what? Trying to calm myself, I drove back to the apartment complex, did a little work, and then picked Grace up after class. And then things calmed down for several months. I was amazed at how little turnover we had. As time went on, I found out that, for the most part, being a landlord was much easier than I thought—*for the most part.*

During calm months we'd go to our day jobs and work, spend weekends trying to improve the appearance of our apartment complex, and then, during off hours, just enjoy ourselves.

From the beginning, I felt that working on the apartments was "for the future." If I remember correctly, when I spent time working on the apartments, I visualized my time as being worth no more than five cents an hour. Better to be earning five cents an hour than paying for entertainment. I vividly remember when I gave myself a raise. My time was now valued at twenty-five cents per hour. At the time, I was making $5.24 an hour on my day job, but most of my contemporaries in college were making at least double, if not many more times, that amount. And, at least a couple making almost $500,000 a year. I was failing, but at least we had a chance.

Recession

And then … and then the world stopped, inflation stopped, vacancies rose—one vacancy, then two. And then, all of a sudden, we had three vacancies, and we were going to be in deep trouble. So I guessed it was time to grow up and get a little competitive. Have you ever seen a grown 30-year-old standing on the sidewalk, holding some helium balloons and a for rent sign while waving to passers-by? If so, that may have been me. I posted signs in convenience stores, in the YMCA, at the co-op—anywhere I could find a board to post a "for rent" notice. I kept making deals and kept filling up units. We kept making our payments. We kept solvent.

The recession was good in some ways. We were still saving Grace's income. Things were under control.

It wasn't too much later that the economy started improving. With an unbelievable amount of luck and good fortune, I survived a round of layoffs. People didn't need help finding jobs so the government didn't need to have people help them. Shortly after that, I became a permanent employee of the State of Washington in the employment office.

Less than two months later, the second round of layoffs got me. I received a letter that said, you are going to be laid off; however, since you are a permanent employee, you have rights. If I had been hit during first round of layoffs, I wouldn't have had any status at all and would have just had to walk out the door. I have no idea what I would have done at that point. I had recovered somewhat from my collapse but not enough to compete. I didn't have the best track record for staying on a job, and I didn't have any job skills. Often in life, it seems, it might be best to ignore all the noise around you and just focus. So, I focused.

The letter instructed me to review the attached list of jobs in the agency and let personnel know if I would qualify and was interested in any job at or below my current salary range. That night, not letting Grace know of the layoff until I had an answer, I sat down and reviewed the options—my options, *our* options. As it turned out, I qualified for 14 jobs at or below my salary level. So, I wrote a letter to central personnel with the list of jobs and asked them to consider me for any job openings.

Within a couple of days, the personnel director called me, and she said, "Ron, I think I have a job for you." The outcome was that I needed to commute an hour each way each day but that I had fallen into a great job—lots of fun and some very enjoyable co-workers.

That had always been my dream job, to do work that I enjoyed, work I understood and could do, and to work with people I enjoyed. I was now even using my degree. I was working in the Statistics and Analysis Unit, State of Washington.

A Big Break

Property management was going reasonably well. The apartment complex was paying for itself. But the work on the complex wasn't easy; nights and weekends weren't easy.

One weekend, after working on and around the complex all weekend, we were driving home. We were crossing the bridge toward home when Grace started to cry, really crying. As we drove on and it got to a place where it was somewhat easy to talk, I asked Grace what was wrong.

To my surprise, she said, "I'm just so happy I get to go to work tomorrow." After a good night's sleep, she was ready to go, and for five days, her life would be predictable as I was the only one "on-call" for whatever happened with the rental during the week.

A short time later, Grace was asked if she was interested in a position as the computer operator trainer for Texaco's East Coast Operations. It would entail traveling to the East Coast a little more than just periodically. It would be a lot of travel and maybe, eventually, even a move. We talked and agreed that she should say, "Yes, interested." If she was hired she'd be making really big money and we'd figure out how to 'make things work'.

Within days, a job as a regional economist for the State of Washington was listed as available. It looked like I qualified for the job. I'm not so sure I would have applied for the job if Grace and I hadn't discussed moving already. I called Grace within minutes of hearing of the opportunity, and we agreed that I should put my name on the list. For one of the few times in human history, a government agency worked faster than a for-profit corporation. I became the regional economist for one of the more remote parts of the state. I was to be assigned to Walla Walla, Washington.

Continuing Forward

In my opinion, optimism is a magnet. In my experience, it usually attracts camaraderie and momentum. There is nothing soft or weak about most optimists. They are usually the ones who laugh at the odds. "What's next?" is the question as they stride into the darkness carrying their own light. Grace and I were and are optimists.

Getting ready to move, we needed to be optimistic. First of all, we needed to figure out what to do with the apartment complex. After all, it was our future. We had survived the downturn, and it was now making money. We liked what the depreciation was doing for our taxes. *What to do?* We decided to run an ad for a resident manager couple in the local newspaper. A small newspaper classified ad—no such thing as Craigslist in

1979. Three couples responded. Only one showed up for the interview. We hired the couple who showed up, Janie and Steve Johnston. Janie and Steve Johnston ended up being the best hires in our career as landlords.

Shortly after Janie and Steve moved into the apartments, I moved to the state's southeastern corner. I rented a room in student housing. I planned to hitch a ride home every Friday evening and then get back to the southeast every Sunday night, usually by Greyhound bus. While home, I'd work with Steve, and I had a married life. Sometimes Grace would ride the bus east, and we'd have a weekend together in Walla Walla. Eventually, I felt reasonably secure in my job, so I started looking at houses. One day I found a house and rented it. Then, within a few months, we had identified enough funds to make a down payment and purchase it.

Now what? We needed to do something with our Tacoma, WA, home and Grace's job.

When we purchased the Tacoma home in 1975, I hoped it would be our "forever home." I was 28 years old, and Grace was 24. We had purchased in a neighborhood of doctors, dentists, attorneys, and small business owners. Way, way over our heads, but Grace and I both really liked the house. Now, having to move east, we considered our options.

We decided to keep the house and rent it out in hopes of returning to it. During a couple of my weekend trips home, I showed the house and eventually rented it to a high-level city employee. Grace was now in a position to move east and join me. The following Monday, Grace gave her notice to Texaco. This time, Texaco offered her a leave of absence, and she took it. She could stay on leave for up to five years.

CHAPTER 8

Living in the East

Once Grace arrived in the southeastern part of the state, things actually started moving along quite well. Even though we were living in a relatively small, rural community, things did happen. Our goods were shipped; we moved them in, mostly to the garage, and Grace started looking for a job.

For perspective, remember Grace grew up on a farm. The event of the year, one event, was the church's annual fundraising festival. That was it. Nothing more than everyday activities day after day, year after year. Not much action on a yearly basis.

On Tuesday of her first week in town, Grace was hired by one of the local banks. She started as a teller. Within a couple of weeks, she was "invited" to bring cookies for the beginning of the month, deposit day, and customer appreciation cookie-fest day. It wasn't really an invitation; it was "expected." Grace, an independent person, didn't appreciate the entire adventure, and being required to come in early but not "clock in" was also a sore point. Additionally, she felt her degree was completely discounted, so the job wasn't working. I decided I needed to see what I could do to help her find a better job.

Looking through want ads, I found one for a customer service job at the local gas company. Bingo. Although she didn't like her job at the bank, she wasn't very excited about going through any more interviews. I had to push her and give her a lot of encouragement, and she did go to the interview. After the interview, I asked her what she thought of the job. She said she thought she would like it "a heck of a lot more than working at the bank." I suggested that she hand-write a "thank-you" note for the interview and tell the hiring manager that she would like the job. She did.

As I expected, Grace got the job. She would be earning twice what she had been earning at the bank. Still not what she was making at Texaco, but a definitive step up.

Three or four months later, a person I interacted with often told me that his boss was looking for a federal grant coordinator, and they hadn't been able to find anyone with anything close to a reasonable background.

Again, I had to push Grace to apply. It was the same old issue, concern about being a "job hopper." I told her that in my experience, being asked to take a job at a higher skill level and with higher pay was not a negative on a vita. Furthermore, no one would ever know if she didn't happen to get the job. Grace did apply, was called, and interviewed. And then everything stopped. We waited. No word.

I decided that the employer didn't want to offer Grace the job for her to turn them down. Walla Walla was a small town, and such events could damage a company's reputation. So, I asked Grace to write a "thank-you" note for the interview and express interest in the job. And, after a little prodding from me, she finally sent it. She got the job and again doubled her pay. Grace was now making close to what she had been making selling tires, batteries, and accessories and as much as her boss at the gas company. And I was making about the same amount as Grace was and had a steady, secure job. As an added bonus, we both had nice co-workers. We were saving money like nobody's business and traveling almost every weekend.

A Baby on the Way

Everything was going quite well, better than ever, truth be known. Jobs, the house, the apartment complex, and we were enjoying the change in scenery. And then, we decided this would be a good time to start a family. After all, we'd been married for over eight years. Very soon, Grace announced we were pregnant. *Great news!*

Winds of Change

Sometimes small things, really relatively small things, really change a person's perspective, their life, and level of enjoyment. Wind changed our life; I know, it was a small thing, but …

After eighteen months of living in the southeastern part of the state, in a small town, I was getting itchy feet. I had always lived in big cities while I was growing up. I loved my job, but I'm a pretty private person, and I do not like going to work on Monday morning and having someone tell me what I did over the weekend. And that was happening regularly. Sometimes the question would be, "We noticed you two were gone for the weekend; where did you go?"

I knew I didn't want to tell anyone I spent my time away pulling weeds, painting walls in apartments, etc. They would have known I/we were crazy. Actually, I didn't want anyone to know we'd invested in an apartment complex. I wanted to do my own "thing." We both did.

For me, the biggest reason for unrest was the weather. I had always been an outside person. Moderate weather was my friend. Think spring, summer, or fall in Seattle, Mountain

View, Santa Barbara, and Inglewood. In the southeastern part of Washington, it was too cold in the winter and much too hot in the summer. Spring and fall lasted all of ten days total, together. So even though I loved my job, overall, things were not great, and I was commuting once or twice a month to Seattle to help Steve and Janie with the apartments, which added even more underlying stress.

And then the wind blew. We'd been in the southeast for over eighteen months, and we had spent little, very little, time outside. One bright early spring day, our opportunity arrived. Grace fixed a fabulous brunch while I set up the outside chairs, the umbrella, and the TV trays so we could sit outside and eat. I set the table and walked into the house to help Grace carry the food to the patio. We put the food on the tables, and I went back into the house to get the salt and pepper. As I walked back out of the sliding glass door, a big gust of wind blew across the deck. The umbrella came down, and the TV trays and food flew away, ending up in the neighbor's yard.

I was fit to be tied. *That was it! The last straw!* Within hours, I told Grace that I wanted to move back to the valley as soon as I could find a job there. At the time, she was seven months pregnant. Grace readily agreed as the idea fit our overall plan of her being a "stay-at-home mother." Life would be easier for us if we were to be in the valley.

Job Hunting and Another Break

There are priorities, and then there are *priorities*. My first priority, as always, was to have a roof over our heads and food on our table. Second, only to that, was for us to be comfortable and enjoy where we were and what we were doing. With those priorities in mind, I started applying for any job I could find that was closer to the state's valley. I probably applied for some twenty jobs, some of which were significant demotions. I did not receive a single call for an interview. Not a one.

Ever alert for possibilities, one day, I found a job announcement for an experimental position. It would be a tremendous promotion for me. It would put me in the top 3 percent of state government employees based on salary. Here I was, at a salary range at which I thought I'd be lucky to retire at, and up pops a chance at a promotion beyond my wildest expectations. I hadn't ever thought to dream that high. *Why not try?*

So I applied. I have always played the "Do not self-eliminate game." I learned at a very young age that if you don't try for something, you are self-eliminating because no one will seek you out.

Some 287 people applied for the plums. There were to be five positions. I made the first cut and was asked to interview. I made the trek to the capital. I remember being quite confident; I knew I was a good interviewee. By now, I had taught thousands of people to interview and write "thank-you" notes. In the end, I was one of the five people chosen for the position. What a shock! I made it farther in my career than I could have ever expected. And then, just five days after reporting to my new job, I was a father. A baby girl (Shirley), and now, more than just being a supportive, maybe even pushy pro-female husband, I became a true feminist. I was set to make sure my daughter, our daughter, was prepared to stand up to anyone.

How did I get "Here"?

Grace and I always wanted me to be around whenever we/she was having a baby. I expected to be shooting buckets waiting for the call to come in and see the baby, but Grace had a different idea. Grace wanted me in the delivery room. We both expected that would happen and, thanks to a good friend and a long labor, it did. The friend, Dan Denver, was one of the friends I made while I had the headhunting job and he had a pilot's license and an airplane.

So, I started my new job in Olympia. It was my third day on the job when Grace called me and told me she had started into labor and was going to the hospital. I told my boss the situation and asked if I could leave.

He said, "Of course."

I then called Dan, with whom I had pre-planned to fly me to Walla Walla. Dan was also the salesperson who found the apartment complex for us. When he said he was available and ready, I called to see when the next Olympia to Tacoma shuttle was leaving. I ran and caught the shuttle; Dan picked me up, we drove to the airport, flew to Walla Walla, and hitch-hiked to the hospital. I ended up getting to Walla Walla some fourteen hours before Shirley was born. She was born shortly after 8 a.m.

We were parents. We spent a short while together, and then I took the car and drove home to continue packing up the house for the move back to Tacoma and my job in Olympia.

CHAPTER 9

Parenting: A Start

I took the rest of the week off to try to be helpful. The doctor kept Grace in the hospital for an extra day, and after that, Grace and Shirley came home. During this time, the world was very aware of a mysterious cause of infant death, sudden infant death syndrome, or SIDS. SIDS was well-documented, and numerous articles had been published on the issue. I was deathly afraid our daughter might die of SIDS. Each night, when Shirley would go to sleep, I was wide awake. I was awake for three straight nights, all night.

On the fourth night, I was in bed and started wondering if I could even think of staying awake for 80+ more nights. SIDS, if it is to happen, usually happens in the first 90 days. I decided to think the issue through. I realized she could die of SIDS, and that was heavy on my mind. However, I realized if she passed that phase, she'd be crawling. Heaven forbid if I forgot to cover one of the electrical sockets. If she survived that phase, then she'd have a bicycle. Someone could back out of a driveway and kill my little girl. Then, if she survived that phase, then by golly, she'd be on a date, and some idiot guy would be driving the car.

Help me.

I decided I couldn't make even a few more nights and definitely not another eighteen years without sleep. I chuckled to myself, rolled over, and went to sleep. Then, forever after, if Grace needed help with any of our kids, she would have to wake me. Unintended consequences.

But that isn't quite the end of that story. When Shirley turned 17, I was looking at my future and started thinking that I wouldn't be responsible for her after her next birthday, when it hit me: she would ALWAYS be my daughter, ALWAYS our daughter, and I would worry about her and care for her for as long as I was alive.

A slow learner I am. A slow learner I am.

Time to Sell the House

Everything was moving quickly, and we had a house to sell. I didn't want to list the house; I just wanted to sell it. So, time to place an ad in the paper. Of course, having a "for sale by owner" house anywhere was not very common in those days; they were usually met with more than a little resistance. By their very nature, FSBO (for sale by owner) threatens a long-standing system. My memory is that we only had one couple show up to view the house. After they had walked through the house, they wanted it. They wanted a house, so their children had a place to grow up. Our house, on a dead-end street, fit the bill.

It was a somewhat sad situation. Shelley, the wife, had a job, but it wasn't producing a lot of money. Her husband, a really quiet guy, was recovering from an on-the-job injury. I can't remember if he was receiving any benefits, unemployment, or workers' comp. That said, Shelley had "that" gleam in her eye. After learning all we could, I told her that if she'd give me $75.00, she could purchase the house over time. I do not remember how we got to that point; however, my guess is that Grace and I were allowed to sell the house per our loan documents. Not sure, maybe not, and maybe I just decided we wanted to sell and did it. At any rate, Shelley gave us $75.00 and moved in a day or two after Grace, Shirley, and I moved back to Tacoma.

The outcome of this $75.00 down payment sale is a great story. Shelley paid every month on time, month after month, after month. Eventually, years later, loan interest rates were low enough that I called her and suggested it might be a good time for them to see if they could get a conventional loan, improve their credit rating and pay us off. She did, and she paid us off. I could not have been more impressed. *What an impressive person!* She knew what she could do, she decided, and she did it.

Refinancing

And then, the payoff for the loan for the apartment complex was looming. Being afraid, I decided to refinance in advance rather than wait until the very last minute. Interest rates were through the roof—the end of the Carter Years. I easily made over 100 contacts, probably closer to 150, looking for a loan. I was begging. I learned ever so much.

When I visited Eagle Mortgage in Meridian, the owner was incredibly nice to me. He told me upfront, "You don't want a loan from me." As we talked, he told me to keep on searching and that I would find a better interest rate than he could afford to give me. He told me that if I didn't find another loan, then I was to come back and see him, and he would give me the loan I needed. I got another education when calling 1-800 toll-free numbers— another fifty inquiries. I was actually put through to a person on one such call and talked with a lender. The conversation stopped when I told them I wanted a $200,000 loan.

After listening to them laugh, I learned that they only did loans for five million and above—way out of our league. Later in life, I learned that I must have contacted a life insurance company. At one point, I entered a building to see a lender and noticed the name "Chuck Lewis" was on the directory. After getting rejected by the lender, I stopped to see Chuck. He was the one who had been nice enough to move my first payment to the end of the purchase agreement. He was one very nice guy and he was pleased that we still had the complex. He suggested I talk with Lincoln Savings and Loan.

I found Lincoln Savings and Loan, and after a bit of begging, I received the funds. The fixed rate on the loan was 14 percent. But, we kept the complex, and it would still be paying for itself. What a journey. But that wasn't the end.

After receiving loan approval, I went to the construction company to pay off the loan, and on their closing document there was a charge for $35,000 for prepayment of the loan. Alas, I called them, asked them to look at the contract, and identified where the attorney had taken out the three words that allowed the prepayment penalty. I had made a great investment in Dale Hermanson. I paid him 75 dollars, and he saved us $35,000—nice ROI (return on investment).

A Duplex

One evening, we received a call from Dan, the pilot and real estate broker who sold us our first apartment complex. He said his broker was getting out of the landlord business and needed to sell a duplex. The broker's wife had been diagnosed with cancer, so it was retirement and liquidation time for them. The broker wanted only the mortgage assumed and enough down payment to cover the closing costs. After inspecting the duplex, even though it was 90 minutes from home, I decided we should buy it, and Grace readily agreed.

A Job for Grace

We had originally planned that we would have four children, and Grace would stay home until the kids were in school. That idea disappeared a couple of months after we moved to Tacoma. One day, I came home from work, and Grace was not her organized self. She was so focused on Shirley that it was apparent that she needed more or at least *some* different stimulation in her days. She had worked since she was 14, so staying at home was a big change. I suggested that she might like to get a part-time job or volunteer now instead of waiting until the kids were school-age. She agreed. She was more than ready.

I started working on this project the very next day. I met with a lot of people at my job, and I mentioned to every single person that Grace was looking for a part-time job. I asked what they knew about part-time jobs. Who did they know? What did they suggest? And on and on. I ended up with a number of possibilities. They ranged from volunteering or applying for jobs within the state system for any part-time jobs "on the board."

There were also part-time jobs at banks and credit unions. The best opportunity appeared to be a part-time accounting clerk position. The position required a minimum of one year of college accounting. Grace had just that and nothing more. The roadblock there was a test in order to qualify. To help Grace get past the roadblock, I visited an accounting professor I had in college and asked him to recommend a book or books that might provide some "quick learning." Instead of recommending a book, he loaned me three books that he felt would "do the trick." Thank you Jack Leonard.

For the next fourteen days, I was the primary care provider the minute I walked in from my day job. Grace studied all evening, every evening, and often well into the night.

There were lots of benefits here. Shirley and I became quite close. Grace, who is a quick study, learned a lot, very quickly. And our world opened up. Grace passed the test, barely, but then how do they address the person who finishes last in a class at a medical school? *Doctor.*

Within a day or two, Grace was hired. No competition for the job. No one wanted a half-time job except us. This was a wonderful opportunity. One of the benefits of this job hunting activity is that we learned of the benefits of a credit union, and we joined one.

Of course, daycare became an issue—an immediate issue. But neither Grace nor I were willing just to accept the status quo. It took us several days to find what we considered to be a reasonable daycare situation. We had to pay for full-time care, but that was just a budgeting issue; we wanted really good daycare.

Grace joined the adult world again and prospered in her job. Over the years, she ended up being offered promotion after promotion. Twice, people in the agency offered her a senior management position. Each time we considered the idea, each time we did the math, and each time we decided the kids were much more important. Grace spent 28 years with the same agency. Always half-time, even with the many promotions.

CHAPTER 10

Hanging On

- *Making things work.*
- *Nights doing paperwork.*
- *Weekends driving 90 minutes to work on one rental and the next weekend driving 45 minutes to work on the other rental.*

Sometimes I went and worked on both rentals on the same weekend. The duplex, for the most part, was easier except when we had quite a bit of occupancy turnover. There is nothing quite like sitting on the stairs, reading a book waiting for someone to read and heed the "for rent" sign, or see the ad and drive over to view the apartment. No cell phones in those days. Interesting times. Lots of learning experiences. And in the evenings during the week, I'd deal with other landlord issues. All the while, we took every opportunity to play.

During this time, I developed a method that worked well for us in dealing with difficult tenants. If a tenant missed a rent payment or was just setting a bad tone for the rental property, I would propose buying them out. I had a day job and didn't have time or the personality to go to court, so buying out someone worked for me.

Being brought up Catholic-military hampered my ability in court (until recently when I finally decided it wouldn't). To the best of my memory, I have been in court four times. I froze each and every time. Sad, but true. Despite my lack of ability, we "won" two out of three times, and the third time we ended up being allowed to evict the tenant who, after the verdict, moved voluntarily. The fourth time, we clearly lost, but it was totally my fault—not a good record. I'm not a quick thinker, and that really hurts in a courtroom. The truth doesn't always win either; that has been true for as long as I have been aware, and the historical record shows much, much longer.

The person with the best attorney wins. The courtroom is not a place for me.

To work around my issues, I paid the first month's rent on a number of storage units for tenants over the years, and we paid for more than a few nights in motel rooms. I also periodically used our little yellow truck to help people move. It all lessened the pressure of any other way to handle the downside of being a property manager. Most of the time, it worked, but there were still times when we got taken.

One of the more interesting move-outs was a time when I was helping a young woman move out of an apartment after I had agreed to pay for her to have both a storage unit and two nights in a local hotel. While I was loading the little yellow truck with her household goods, her out-of-control boyfriend showed up. As he was yelling at me and walking up the stairs to see her, the drawer I was carrying slipped a little in my hands, and suddenly, a number of unused bullets showed in the corner of the drawer. I was sure the boyfriend was going to come down the stairs with a loaded gun and that I was going to die. Pure and simple. *What a way to go.*

To my great relief, the two of them walked down the stairs, and she kissed him, and they left; he walked away like a little lamb. *Whew.*

A Real Safety Net

At about this time, while we were visiting Grace's family in Kentucky, my father-in-law stopped the tractor and offered us the greatest safety net ever. WIt happened while we were taking a break from the harvesting we were doing. My father-in-law, Henry Blewett, was a very quiet person. He would mull things over for long periods until he found something he thought might work. I could tell he had thought out his idea and done some research. He and I got along quite well, and I am sure that helped. I came to town during harvest season every few years, and neither of his boys or any of the other sons-in-law were around. That helped too.

My father-in-law told me that he had checked all the laws, rules, and regulations and that if at any point in time the economy or any mistake I made was so bad that my family needed refuge, he could put another house on the farm. He said, "I wish you all the best, but I know things happen. If one of those things happens to you, then you are welcome here."

I couldn't think of much more than to say than, "Thank you."

Then Henry said, "Let's get back to work."

The whole concept hit me. That evening I thought about it and realized what a great gift he'd given my family and me.

I was impressed with Henry, as usual, and over-joyed for our family. What a great show of support.

You Can't Read

After we moved near to the Sound, it became clear that I needed a new optometrist. Much to my surprise, during my appointment, the doctor told me I couldn't read. I listed off for him my emotional foxhole, my mantra of my accomplishments. He told me quite bluntly that he didn't care what I'd accomplished; I couldn't read. I told him I'd had my eyes checked almost every year since I was five, and his news was really quite a shock.

He asked about my reading habits, and I told him I didn't read very much. "I only read one complete textbook in college. When I read, it took about fifteen minutes before I got a headache. I always figured that other people just put up with the headaches more than I was able to put up with them."

He laughed; I asked for a second opinion. He referred me to another recent graduate, and alas, I had to admit, I couldn't read. After this, Shirley and I spent many an hour in the family room doing eye coordination exercises. The exercises paid off for me with number of benefits. After a few weeks of vision therapy, I started reading, and to this day, I read almost every day. I so enjoy having the ability to read. Short term, I was able to read a lot more. Long term, my relationship with Shirley has held. As my eyes got weaker and weaker in later years, I finally agreed to accept prisms in my lenses. Once again and again, I was a lucky guy.

A Second Child, May 1982

In the midst of all of this, our second child came along, Sam. Sam was a little bowling ball, stocky and solid, with a great smile. Lots of fun. To this day, he and I seem to enjoy getting together. We have taken a number of road trips together, and he has helped me see the world. He is a good friend, and if I ever got myself into a real pickle, I'd want him to be with me. We'd figure a way out.

A Walk to Remember

Not so many years later, our two kids were really growing. Sam could talk and walk; Shirley, our firstborn, was old enough to use the phone to call for help if she needed any. Additionally, we had two extremely nice neighbors who would have done anything to assist Shirley if she needed any type of help. So, Grace and I started walking in the evenings to help with our health and to reduce some of the stress we felt each day. Neither of us believed in watching television, and we figured we would just run across any really important news while we were on our day jobs, so finding the time to walk was easy. Nice walks. All right in our neighborhood. All less than a 2- or 3-minute jog from the house.

One evening we were walking and talking about our investments, and it became apparent that the duplex was a real drag, a drain, mostly a time drain but also a physical drain. Grace was somewhat interested in selling it. I told Grace that the duplex was underwater, and we owed more than it was worth. It was cash flowing quite nicely, but we owed more than it was worth. She and I then speculated that our grandkids would probably have to sell the duplex if we were ever going to make any real money out of it. The economy looked that bad. We decided to hold onto the duplex. We'd just need to hang on long enough, but, from the looks of things, it could be a long, long time.

The Storm

We lived in a part of the country that enjoyed pretty moderate weather, year-round, year after year—lots of rain but very few days of snow or ice. Then there was the shocker that closed down much of the state. Snow, ice, and all that goes with them. It closed almost everything. Very few people were on the street—almost no one on the freeways.

We received a call around 6 a.m. one morning, if not a whole lot earlier. I was told that water was flooding the apartment complex's basement storage. The water was backing up in the storage/laundry room. The room had at least *three feet* of water in it. And the water was continuing to back up and get deeper. I looked out and realized there wasn't any way for me to get on the road and get all the way to the apartment complex, and even if I was able to get there, I didn't have any idea what I should do or where the water shut-off might be. Back on the phone.

I don't know how many calls I made that morning. Looking at the phone bill, I'd suspect 70 or more long-distance calls, but most of the plumbing shops were closed. But just when I was nearly exhausted, I hit a home run. I found a plumber who was at home and he lived about two blocks from the apartment complex. He agreed to walk over and deal with the issue.

By the time he arrived, the water was over five feet deep in the basement. He found the water's main shut off, drained the basement, found that one of the faucets had swelled when the water had turned to ice, and he fixed the faucet, and then turned the water back on. I don't remember what he charged us. I do remember that the price was unbelievably low considering what it was worth to us and what I thought it would be. *How lucky can a person be?*

CHAPTER 11

A New to Us Home

Grace was pregnant again. Our house was small and really only had two bedrooms. We had made a makeshift bedroom for Sam, but he was quickly out-growing it. Time to move. Time to make a list. Grace ended up with a list of 22 features she would like to have in a new house. She'd always been a neighborhood shopper. Being a neighborhood shopper made home-buying easier for us—fewer options but more that are close to what we are targeting.

Eventually, after six or seven months of watching her neighborhoods and choosing a real estate agent to represent us, we received a call. A house had just come on the market, and apparently, it had 20 of the 22 "features" Grace wanted. Grace scurried over, looked at it, and verified it had almost everything she wanted. Grace wanted the house. That was enough for me. Fortunately, it was underpriced. We needed to sign an earnest money agreement as soon as possible. Three hours later, we had signed the earnest money agreement, and the sellers had signed it too.

This ended up being a slightly longer process than we had come to think of as a usual and customary residential closing. At one point, the sellers were ready to back out. I was in their kitchen talking with them. Grace was there too; she was crestfallen. I asked why they wanted out of the earnest money. It turned out that an entity that was making the loan required a fee of $25.00 from the seller. I don't remember what it was for, but we, the buyers, couldn't legally pay it for them as there was some law that prevented that possibility. I spotted a spoon on the counter and asked if I could purchase it for $25.

The husband looked at me wide-eyed and seemed somewhat shocked. Then, realizing I was serious, he looked at his wife, held up the spoon, smiled, and then they both looked at me and said, "Yes." A few days later, we had a new house in a neighborhood Grace liked, and I feared. We both ended up being "right."

A Third Child

Days after closing in April, we had our third child. A beautiful baby girl, Marilyn. In the beginning she was a very fussy baby. For her first 88 days, I often held her over my head with my arms outstretched to help her and quiet her. She had colic, and whenever her tummy hit my stomach, it hurt her. She was our rebellious one, but she has turned out to be a wonderful young woman and, at the time of this writing, has become a new mother. Grace and I both look forward to being a part of her and her family's life for years to come. *What a thrill to have a grand-daughter!* Janine

The Beach, A Condo

Tent camping is fun, right? Well, a lot of the time, tent camping is fun. I happen to really enjoy it. Before Marilyn, our little family would camp on the Washington Coast a couple of times, sometimes three or four times, a summer. We also camped on our long road trips back and forth, to and from, Kentucky. We had been toying with getting a cabin in the mountains or a place at the beach for some time. Shortly after Marilyn was born, we found a condo on a high beach on the Washington Coast. Grace was excited as she hated wet campsites, and beach camping was frequently wet.

I'm sure it didn't help that we went beach camping when Sam was an infant. One time, it had rained the night after we set up the tent, and it was periodically raining the next day. Shirley and I would get out of the tent and play when it wasn't raining, and sometimes I would carry Sam with me. Grace did not enjoy it. Our having fun while dealing with the circumstances didn't help things at all. Grace really didn't want to go through anything near the same thing again with Marilyn as an infant.

Since we enjoyed the coast so much we decided to look for a place at the beach. We looked at single-family dwellings and condos. We focused on properties that might make us some money. We knew ourselves well enough that if we didn't own, we would have a difficult time "throwing away the money" just renting a hotel room for a night or two now and then. Just two grown-ups, afraid of being poor and trying to live with themselves and within their budget.

After reviewing the rules and regulations and method of distributing income for six or seven of the condo associations we liked, we purchased a beachfront one-bedroom, one-bath condo. The long-term outcomes of this purchase are:

(a) We never camped on the Washington Coast again.

(b) We rarely stayed in the condo so as not to let it lose income.

We did stay enough that we developed a lot of nice patterns and made a lot of sand castles. *Fun!* Almost 35 years later, we still own the condo. Claire and her husband use the condo quite a bit; so do Shirley and her husband, and so do I. We took the condo out of the rental pool so that any portion of the family could use it at any time desired. It has all worked out.

We bought the condo on contract because, in those days, it was almost impossible to get financing for a condo. We were in the association's rental pool for most of the time we have owned, but we did, for about five years, try to rent the condo on our own. This was in the early days before Airbnb, and it wasn't easy, so we eventually migrated back to the rental pool. Knowing thyself is, in my opinion, one of the keys to investing; luckily, we knew who we were when we purchased the condo.

Economy Surges

One year, out of nowhere, the economy began to surge. The duplex, a strain on our lives, was, all of a sudden, worth a lot of money. Unbelievable, absolutely unbelievable. *Time to sell.* I mentioned this desire to Dan, the friend who sold us the apartment complex and had suggested we purchase the duplex. He and another friend had set up their own residential real estate company, and I decided he might have some idea of how to go about selling the duplex. As it turned out, his partner was looking for an investment property and decided to purchase the duplex. Now we had to decide to either take the money or do a tax-free 1031-real-estate exchange. We chose to take the exchange route.

The Apartment Complex from Hell

Next question: *Where to exchange?* The Washington economy was booming, so there didn't seem to be any reasonable options there. So, we decided to look at California. For whatever reason, the California economy was lagging, so there were real estate deals to be made there. I decided it would be nice if we could find an apartment complex near where my parents lived. So, I focused my research on Southern California. Eventually, after submitting some 25 or 30 offers, we had three accepted offers. I flew to Los Angeles, rented a car, visited my parents, and reviewed the three properties. We decided on a nice-looking 24-unit apartment complex in Oceanside, California, and we closed and started looking for a property manager.

Before I go further, you need to know two things:

First, I had done my numbers extremely conservatively. I put high vacancy numbers on my spreadsheet; I overestimated any expenses that were reported. The numbers were extremely conservative.

Second, our goal was to have a property manager manage the property and for me to fly to the area twice a year to check on it and make sure the property manager was doing a reasonable job, then see my parents and fly home.

Despite my best efforts and those of the property managers, everything was out of control very quickly and probably had been for some time. The manager could not keep the gates and grounds operating well, could not track down skippers, rarely, if ever, collected a full month of rent payments, and just couldn't gain control of the property. The fact is that over the next 21 months, none of the four property managers I hired could get the complex under control.

At one point, I was walking with the fourth property manager and trying to figure out the problem, and he said to me, "Didn't anyone ever tell you that Oceanside is the flake capital of the world?"

The conversation made me even more concerned than I had been before taking the most recent trip.

Each and every month, Grace and I were losing more money than both of us made, combined. I wasn't flying to SoCal twice a year; I was flying to SoCal every six weeks, once a month, then finally every other week.

Palm Springs California

While in the process of exchanging and purchasing the "Complex from Hell," we ended up with something just less than $11,500 in the exchange fund. I advocated for taking the money and paying taxes on it. I was exhausted and personally and physically over-extended.

Grace had another idea. A few years earlier, we had taken our three kids on a road trip for spring break. We traveled to and throughout Arizona and had a wonderful time exploring that state. On our drive back to Washington, we happened to stop and camp on a lake outside Palm Springs, California.

Now, with $11,500 in our pocket, Grace suggested that we should purchase a place in Palm Springs. She reasoned that we bought rentals, but, "Let's buy one we can sometimes enjoy and maybe where we can retire someday." I made several calls and ended up talking with a real estate agent in Palm Springs who I felt possibly understood our needs and desires. He verified that Palm Springs, like the rest of California, was in recession. Then, he sent us paperwork on over thirty properties for us to review. Grace and I sat up in bed a couple of, maybe even a few, nights, reviewed all the properties, and ranked them based on what we read.

We then scheduled for me to fly to Palm Springs on a weekend, review properties, and make an offer. During the first two days of my trip, the real estate agent and I looked at over thirty condos. Sitting in the local Burger King Sunday night, I reviewed my notes and wrote up nineteen offers. The less I liked the property, the larger difference I offered between the asking price and my offer. Monday morning, I gave the offers to the real estate agent, and I flew back to work.

By the end of the week, we had sixteen turndowns, and three accepted offers. The next weekend, Grace flew to Palm Springs, reviewed the three properties, and decided which one she wanted. We ended up with a great unit. Grace did a good portion of her validation by asking and knowing how the sun would arc each quarter of the year. That condo is still in our family and is still used in the winter and any other times that family members are nearby. That provides a lasting positive for what we went through with the Complex from Hell.

CHAPTER 12

A Way Out of Hell

Sometime after one of my returns from Oceanside, California, to Washington, a real estate agent called me from SoCal. The agent asked if we would be willing to sell the Oceanside apartment complex. I tried to hide my readiness, told him we might be willing to sell, and asked what he had in mind. He said he was working with a well-off investor who wanted to accumulate property in southern California. So we agreed to meet on my next trip to SoCal.

Soon after I landed in SoCal, the agent and I met, and he presented the offer. That evening I called Grace and told her we should sell. The offer would get us out of the complex, pay us back all of the money we had slammed into the complex and make us a few bucks. We could avoid bankruptcy. I couldn't believe the offer.

We took the offer, closed on the property, and went through another tax-free exchange. Unbelievable! As I watched the SoCal market surge, I was sure the buyer made a lot of money, but for us, we had stopped the hemorrhaging.

Apartment Complex +

The exchange property ended up being a 24-unit apartment complex in Tacoma, WA, along with an adjoining old house on a large lot.

Fired

Okay, I wasn't *technically* fired, but I was fired. For whatever reason, it happened; now it was time for some budget cuts. I had heard rumors, but frankly, I had other issues on my mind. This time I got caught in the cuts instead of being part of the team implementing the cuts. I am sure this was the fourth round of budget cuts in recent years, maybe even the fifth round. I had made some management mistakes, had a "friend" undercut me, saw things I didn't like, and reported them. And I was a poor manager. All of it made me vulnerable. I deserved to be fired; *being cut* was a much better option.

Some interesting things happened in relatively short order. First, I was cut. Then, the head honcho, Dr. Joe, who people told me had played himself in the movie, *One Flew Over the Cuckoo's Nest,* when he worked in Oregon, decided he would red-line the salary of every employee cut, including mine. That meant that his agency would be keeping my salary at the before-the-cut level until my new position, whatever that might be, reached the same salary level—a great break for Grace and me.

As it turned out, my immediate boss decided to ignore me, and so other than occupying a position, I was expected to sit in a room and do nothing. He would not give me any work or allow anyone in the section to give me any work. From what I learned as time went on was that he thought ignoring me would motivate me to quit.

So, what to do? First of all, I would apply for jobs that I'd like. I decided that while waiting for interviews, I'd try to get caught up on my real estate paperwork where I was getting far behind. I had enough of that to keep me busy for quite a while. After that, I'd see what else I could do. One step at a time, one foot in front of the other.

As this unfolded over the next thirty months or so, lots of positives happened. I had our real estate records in reasonable order for what would eventually appear to be the last time. I had two new bosses above me. The main one in my line, two above me, decided to give me a job, and then he tried to really fire me. This ended up being a very good education for me as I learned to really manage an adverse situation. As it turned out, my new immediate boss decided I had real value. My new immediate boss gave me some interesting spreadsheets to work on, and although I felt underutilized, I really did enjoy the work.

My immediate boss, who seemed really squared away, left the organization before I did because he could not believe how political state government and state government jobs could be. When I finally left the organization, his boss, the boss who had tried to fire me, stopped me in the hallway and congratulated me on the fine work I had been doing with the organization's many spreadsheets—quite a victory for me mentally. It was a nice feeling to have turned that corner and the relationship around. That was very mature of you, Johnny Morgan. I was very impressed.

Trying Again

Soon after I was "cut" from my exalted position, I decided to try my possibilities in the financial services industry, selling life insurance, property insurance, annuities, and mutual funds during my personal time. A short while later, I started applying for higher positions within the state system. In the past, I had interviewed seven times in the state system, won all seven positions, and been hired seven times in a row. I figured I would be hired again right away. As it turned out, it would be almost three years before I did find a "better" job. That said, I enjoyed doing spreadsheets, working on real estate, and trying to build a second business, the insurance business, on the side, so the time flew by.

The Pediatricians Are Moving

Over the years, our children received wonderful pediatric care. Liking your doctor is a real plus, and we did. With three kids, we were able to really get to know the members of one of the local pediatrician groups quite well.

One day, we had to see the pediatrician for one of the kids. While there, the doctor mentioned to me that the pediatric group was trying to sell their building, but no one had made an offer. That evening, after reviewing what I thought could happen with the building, I worked up an offer. Grace consented, and shortly after, we owned a medical building on one of the most important corners in the entire town. The building was old, and it was ugly. It had lots of problems, but the location was fantastic, and I knew it had potential. I had often read the mantra "Location, Location, Location." We made the offer, it was accepted, and we closed on the property.

The plumber that helped me with the building was a Korean War vet who was almost retired. He was smart and fun and really knew "his stuff." One day, we were working on a project in the main part of the building, and as we walked by the main office, I introduced him to the front office staff. I told them, "His name is Bill Moore, but I've always wished it was Bill

Less." The front office staff laughed, and he joined in. I'm sure he ended up telling that story to almost as many people as I did. Nice guy.

Vacant Lots

As time wore on, we continued to accumulate cash. Then, out of the blue, a real estate agent contacted me and suggested that he had an investment we might want to consider. This had become quite common for me, but for some reason, this one felt "right," and it was in our price range and easy for me to "check out."

Eventually, we ended up purchasing the property, which included two vacant lots—two of the few vacant lots still available on a major artery leading into the city. The seller wanted to sell, we wanted to buy, and the agent wanted it to sell so much that he cut his commission to make the deal work. Location, location, location.

Over the next several years, we would have the lots mowed whenever the City informed us they needed to be mowed. Overall, pretty low maintenance.

Another Vacant Lot

A few years later, another vacant lot came available. This one was next to the apartment complex and old house we already owned. The developer needed to sell the lot, so we were offered to purchase it at what we thought was a really good price for us, so we ended up buying it too.

A New Job for Me

One evening while at my day job, I just got a little frustrated. After three years of searching, it was obvious that my reputation had been tarnished, and my "luster" was gone. I'd probably interviewed for seven or eight jobs and only got to the second round twice. There must be something I could do that would make me feel better about who I was, what I was doing. Frustrated, I walked out of my office and down the hall to stretch and get a little exercise. While in the hall, I noticed the department's job announcement clipboard. I don't remember having ever looked at it before, but I could be wrong.

Alas, there was a job announcement at my pay grade, running a calculator, and the job was half-time. Interesting. It took me about 10 minutes to decide to go for the job. I was mentally, and I thought financially, ready for half-time. Grace agreed. It didn't take too long, and I was selected for the job—what a relief. I felt great about the whole thing; what I'd be doing, my new co-workers, and especially my new job share partner, Cathrine. Cathrine was on her way "home" to have her first of what ended up being two delightful young women.

So now, Grace and I were both working half-time. This would be useful over the next seven and a half years as we worked around school schedules, sick kids, business, and the like. I enjoyed that job quite a bit. Nice boss, nice co-workers. I was negotiating with attorneys who wanted to do indigent defense work for the state. The surroundings make all kinds of difference. And after I did the bean counting, I would travel to various counties and negotiate. *How cool, a job with paid travel. I could learn about the state. How lucky can I be?*

As I look back, I missed a pretty good opportunity; I could have been looking for investment-grade real estate while I was on the road. But, ah, I was just enjoying everything.

CHAPTER 13

A Memory, A Goal

Here we were, Grace and I, both working half-time, then I'd head home, do some financial counseling and life insurance sales, and work on the rentals. Grace would head home from her job, take care of the kids, and then do the books for the rentals. We'd trade off taking care of the kids on sick days and teacher education days.

One day, as I was walking from my daytime office to the credit union during my morning break, I realized that I was going to deposit the entire gross income from the rentals. I had just over $3,850 in my hand. We weren't netting very much from the rentals, but everything we did net, we put against whatever mortgage had the higher interest rate and no prepayment penalty. We both knew that credit card debt was the beginning of the end. I don't think that, even in the worst of times, we ever let credit card debt roll over from one month to the next unless it was a 0-percent card. As I walked along, I told myself that we should continue working on rentals until we could deposit $3,850 each week—a goal that just popped into my brain.

Why don't we shoot to be able to deposit $3,850 into the credit union each and every week of the year, 52 weeks a year? Now, some 30 years later, as we are depositing over five times that amount each day, that goal seems pretty modest. At the time I made it, it seemed almost unattainable.

An Audiotape, "Money – The Basics"

Trying to make real money, once again. It is not that I wasn't busy. I was taking care of rentals and had three enjoyable children and a nice wife, but I wanted to be "successful." So, I decided to put together an audiotape. "Money - The Basics" was born. I wrote it and recorded it. This new venture upset Grace because she couldn't understand how I felt I could carve out time for such a venture. Alas, I could not figure out how to market the audio tape. I am sure that made Grace even more upset.

I sold a number of copies but just enough to maybe cover the costs, definitely not much more. Several people told me how good it was. One family actually tracked me down and thanked me for saving their late 20's son from spending himself into oblivion. I still have 8 to 12 copies of it. I hand one out every now and then when I find someone who I think has some potential, is motivated, and wants to learn. It made me feel good, but in the final analysis, it was yet another bust for me.

Another Fantastic Opportunity, But ...

Another great opportunity was when an owner of one of the three largest property and casualty agencies in Tacoma asked if I would want to sell annuities and life insurance for his entire book of business. I liked Dave Muench, the owner, and thought we could make a good team. I was so optimistic that

Grace and I traded half of the pediatric building for half of Dave's insurance office building. I believe that every insurance agent you would talk with would tell you that this was a multi-million dollar opportunity. I started working on the book of business.

I failed. I still haven't learned how to sell *anything*, except vacancy. I can fill a vacant apartment or a vacant office space with the best of them. So far, I cannot sell. I will have to explore that opportunity.

Then everything started falling apart. David was a handy person. I am not. People who know me don't trust me with hammers or screwdrivers. I would deal with tenants and tenant issues. Then, as needed, I'd ask Dave for help with projects. Grace kept the books. In the meantime, during the midst of all of this, David confides in me that he is now a millionaire. Quite unfortunately, in lots of ways, this changed Dave. He decided he was doing too much of the work. His personality changed to haughty. Sadly, this ruined not only our relationship but also his marriage, and because the people working for him didn't like the new "Dave," they basically stole his entire book of property and casualty business, over seventy percent of it and started their own agency.

Just before his world really started crumbling, Dave and I tried to work things out. Unfortunately, we could not come to terms but were able to just undo the property trade, and that was the end.

SWAT Team

At 6:30 one morning, I answered the phone: "Mr. Gibson, I need to tell you that a SWAT team has just broken into your house across the street."

What? What to do? I decided just to wait to see who would call me to tell me what had happened. The house was less than a mile away, but there wasn't much I could do at the scene, so I decided just to continue forward.

Eventually, someone from the police department called late in the day and told me there had been drug activity and drug selling out of the house. The tenant had been taken to jail. The funny thing was, I had spent three or four evenings working in the house during the previous three weeks to try and fix some of the cold air leaks. I'd probably spent six or more hours in the house and hadn't noticed anything. I know I am naïve, but this really pointed it out to me. As it turned out, a relative of the now former tenant showed up, took care of the kids, and removed all of the personal belongings. It was a nice easy turnover.

The last laugh for me came two months later while I was still working on renting the house. The now-former tenant, who was just released from jail, called and left me a voicemail. She said, "Mr. Gibson, I know I have caused you some problems, but would you please rent one of your apartments to me?"

That was perhaps the very first call that I never returned. At least that time, a new management idea came out of the incident: not returning useless calls. I still probably return many more phone calls than I should, but that is because a person never knows what opportunities are out there and coming at you. So I answer the phone and return most calls. It is an opportunity expense.

Our First Million

And then it happened; our net worth reached *one million dollars*. It somehow snuck up on us. I had been doing a net worth calculation every six months, but with life swirling around us, I'd missed making a calculation or two, and we had quite a bit of growth in the preceding twelve months. We talked about it for a few minutes. When we started, we had wondered if we'd ever reach the goal. And here we were, we were millionaires! And then, later that night, Grace was doing the books, and I was planning the weekend's work.

Fire

"Ron, there is a fire at your apartment complex."

Yikes! Guess I should get there. I arrived and found the fire was already out. Great work by the fire department. As it turned out, the resident whose unit was on fire had fallen asleep while smoking. A neighbor, a guy who had all kinds of personal potential, had seen the fire from his window. He ran out the door, smashed open the neighbor's door, grabbed the still sleeping neighbor, and saved a life.

I had seen the rescuer a few times; I worked around the apartments a lot. He was a nice person and had a nice small family. In my opinion, he had so much potential. I just hated to see him throwing all that potential away. I was ready to pay for him to have his teeth fixed and send him to counseling. But, alas, he was too afraid and turned me down. So very, very sad. Wasted potential. Los of people just disqualify themselves. Reasons unknown.

CHAPTER 14

"Retirement," October 1997

Time flies. I'm six months from 50. Wow. How could I be "that" old? At any rate, I really wanted to retire and do it at age 49, plus maybe 300 days—just ego. I was excited to be able to tell people I retired at 49. My boss allowed me to work half-time for seven and a half years. At any time, she could have made my job full-time and forced me to make a decision, leave or work full-time. She never forced me to make that decision. Half-time allowed me to help care for my children and work on our rentals. By this time, I knew I couldn't support my family selling insurance. Another failure, but I had to accept it. That said our real estate numbers worked for me to stop my day job.

So, with six months to go, I gave my notice. A couple of weeks later, my boss called me into her office and requested that I stay on the job for an extra six months. Angela Christiansen, my boss, had been so good to me. She told me she just didn't have time to hire a replacement for me. I was pretty sad but had to agree to stay on the job for the extra six months. I had to stay. It was time for me to give back. No big deal, considering all Angela had done for my family and me.

Starting on a Future

Lou Cotton, my swimming pool friend of long ago, and I had kept in touch over the years. We climbed mountains together and had lunch together often. He has remained a very nice guy and a good friend. One day, when I was scheduled to be in Seattle, I asked him if he'd like to have lunch. We went to lunch, and I told him I was retiring. We talked for a long time during that lunch. A few days later he called me and asked if I would help him find a place to lease for his business. His business had grown; he couldn't expand in his current location and needed something much larger. I agreed to start looking as I had time.

Selling "The House" – Part 1

My retirement checks would not start for four and a half years after retiring. The answer to the income gap was to sell our dream house in Seattle. This was our "forever house," the one we left when we moved to southeastern Washington. It was not an easy decision. We had only lived in the house for a couple of years. We both loved the house. The kids even knew the house, as one or two of them would join me at the house when we had a rental turnover. Shirley and I both remember one such turnover where she joined me and sat in the beautiful bay window on a warm sunny afternoon doing homework while I worked to clean up and re-rent the house.

Shirley and Sam probably both remember spreading bark dust and doing yard work there. Marilyn was too young to make any of the turnover trips and probably only remembers the house from an occasional drive-by to review it years later. To this day, Grace and I drive by it every few years. It was a house "to remember." At any rate, we sold the house on a lease option. It appeared to me to be a clean deal. I sold it with a really good price and great terms for the buyer, and we didn't need to deal with the house anymore, or so I thought.

As the months went by, payments were getting later and later. It felt like a drippy faucet, and then it stopped. I could not talk the tenant into leaving. It really was an interesting case to me. Why would the tenant start making improvements and stop making payments with such a good deal at stake? He had put thousand dollars into fixing up the house. In the evenings, when we met, I could tell that he and his family lived there, and they were living well, but we still could not make a plan for him to catch up on payments. Actually, it looked like it would be a long time before he could make payments at all— they were living well above their means. And, no matter what I offered to do for him and his family, he would not agree to move.

For the first time in years, I decided I needed to go through the eviction process. I feared going to court because you never know which judge you will get and how "justice" might work out. My case was the first on the docket. I stood up and told the judge my side of the issue, and the judge asked, "Is the tenant here?"

I hadn't seen the tenant come in, but he was, indeed, in the courtroom. So the tenant sauntered to the front railing in the court, and while walking, he said, "Your Honor, I will need at least a month to move."

The judge looked at the tenant, snarled, and said, "Mr. Smith, you will be out by Monday, 5 p.m., or I will have the locks changed and have you picked up and hold you in contempt."

That was it. Tuesday morning, I drove to Seattle, and the house was basically empty; the keys were on the kitchen counter. Sometimes I just don't understand.

Selling "The House" - Part 2

Now to sell the house, again. That day, Tuesday, I started cleaning out the house, vacuuming, and picking up wood and nails from the former tenant's projects. In general, I was just trying to make the house presentable for an open house so we could sell it.

On the third open house weekend, I had two interested prospects. Shirley had made brownies, and that made the house smell like a home. I eventually used nice, inviting, comforting smells to sell a number of houses.

I followed up with the two prospects and gave them more information about the house and neighborhood. One of the prospects fell by the wayside after a couple of short discussions, but the other really seemed to want the house. Jon, the prospect, and I negotiated for over two months. By this time, I knew his wife, Chris, really wanted the house. It was that obvious. She was much younger than Jon, very good-looking, and full of energy.

Additionally, I knew Jon owned a very large engineering company in Seattle. He and I ended up having an enjoyable time negotiating. He'd give me a scenario; I'd give him a price and terms. After about five tries at doing this, he said to me, "Ron, every time we discuss an idea, the numbers always work out, so you end up getting the same amount of money for the house."

Jon eventually purchased the house. He gave me something like $10,000 down, then financed pretty soon after that and paid us off. Once it started moving, it all moved quickly. Jon and I stayed in touch until he died. Nice guy and, for many years, quite a water polo referee.

David's IRS Debt

Remember David Muench, my business partner and friend, who owned the insurance company? Well, about this time, I received a call from the IRS collections department. They were getting ready to lien the pediatric building and wondered if I wanted to pay the debt before they put the lien on the property.

What? Well, as it turned out, I hadn't wanted to waste the $25.00 recording fee, so the infamous "re-trade" never showed up on county records. Alas, the IRS thought David still owned half of the pediatric building. Actually, the IRS was very cooperative. We were able to find the telephone log showing the talk about the re-trade, and we had the deed turning the pediatric building back to us. It was a good deed. Definitely a good deed. It shouldn't have appeared fake because it wasn't. A pretty big adrenalin spike, but it all turned out. We must have passed the burden-of-proof test, so this issue disappeared—no foul, almost no harm. I told David about this a couple of years later when I ran into him at an art fair. He was now back to being the great guy I thought he was, and we shared quite a laugh about what happened. To this day, I like Dave Muench.

A Note about the IRS

I have had four "encounters" with the IRS. I guess I should say, "so far." There was the one noted above. One was about five or six years after we purchased our first rental. Another was a dispute about bark dust at rental #1 or #2. And the fourth was about "excessive write-offs" at rental #1. Regarding the last three, I always tell people, "I won one, lost one, and tied one." All, to me, are stories worth telling. The IRS employees across the board have always been more than professional in every encounter.

1. The IRS contacted us when Grace was 8.75 months pregnant with Shirley, and I had just accepted the job in Olympia.

I went in for the meeting and told the interviewer we were packed and ready to move. The interviewer said the IRS would move the file to Olympia. After Shirley was born and we had moved, I contacted the IRS in Olympia, and they, indeed, had the file. As it turned out, many months later, after discussions between Darryl Houck and the IRS, Darryl told me to pay. Darryl was upset and not quite sure the IRS was reading correctly, but he had pleaded his case as far along as reasonable. *Time to pay.*

According to the IRS, Darryl had written off, rather than depreciating the appliances in the 14-unit apartment complex. The golden liner here was that it would have been very difficult, if not all but impossible, for us to pay our IRS bill at any time after closing and the ensuing eighteen months or more. However, at the time of the settlement with the IRS, almost seven years later, we could afford to pay. Am I/are we lucky? A loss but sustainable.

2. I met with the IRS in Olympia. The issue was "bark dust" and if we should claim it as an expense or depreciate it.

The expense was something like $250. I just agreed to depreciate it. Darryl was upset with me but I told him that I just wanted to get out of the IRS office. Catholic-military I am. A tie.

3. Was about excessive expense write-offs.

As usual, Grace and I, two pretty fearful people, were both very scared of my pending meeting with the IRS. We both pulled our tax backup records. She worked upstairs in the dining room, and I was working while lying on the sofa in the family room. Marilyn was probably four, so I'm guessing it was 1990 or so. Grace and I reviewed and reviewed. We could not find anything.

Finally, we went to the actual receipts, and again, nothing—back to our calculations. We lined them up side by side on a spreadsheet. And there it was, staring at us: *my error*.

It turned out she had put a $1,500 expense on her spreadsheet; I did not see that expense during my review and there, on my paperwork, was an added expense of $1,500. *What to do?*

Well, Darryl had always told me never to volunteer anything when talking with the IRS. So, on the day of my appointment, I went from my state office to the IRS and sat and trembled, waiting for my appointment. When called in, I was greeted by the IRS agent, and I sat across the desk from him. He asked for my records. I handed him the apartment expense envelope. A standard business envelope stuffed with receipts. He looked through about twenty receipts, then pulled one out and asked me, "Is this a receipt for 5 dollars or 500 dollars?"

More than nervously, I said, "I wish I could tell you that was 500 dollars, but that is 5 dollars."

At this time, he folded the envelope and told me that he recommended that we separate our expense receipts by category in the future. He then handed me the envelope and stood up, we shook hands, and I left—a win.

Don't be too afraid of them but don't talk any more than you must.

SECTION 3

Over the TOP

An Unbelievable Journey

CHAPTER 15

The Cotton-Gibson Building

Lou Cotton

People often ask Lou or me what led us to agree to own a business splitting it exactly in half; Lou owns half, and I own the other half. The truth is we did this despite an attorney's recommendation not to do it.

Well, you need to know a little about our history to understand, so let me tell you about Lou Cotton. Lou grew up on a farm in northern Washington State. He attended college at one of the Washington State regional colleges, Central Washington; if I am remembering correctly, he majored in geography. Upon graduation, he worked some jobs, including selling insurance, and eventually became a supervisor at a trucking company. While at the trucking company, he decided he didn't like how his life was playing out and decided he would like to be a dentist. In order to get into dental school, he needed more hard science courses, so he enrolled at the University of Washington, sold his house, and moved to an apartment complex. As mentioned before, he and I met in the swimming pool at that very apartment complex.

Sometime later, his younger brother, Don, accompanied us on one of our mountain climbs. Unfortunately, Don forgot his gloves for the climb. My fingers have always been very cold on climbs, so I had double layers of gloves. I loaned one pair of my gloves to Don. About 9,000 feet up, the three of us had to cross a sheer wall of ice. We roped up, put on our crampons, picked up our ice axes, and started across. Being the oldest, I was in the middle of the rope. About two-thirds of the way across the ice wall, my fingers froze, and I could no longer use my ice ax, so I was in trouble. Lou and Don both inched toward me, ended up massaging my hands, and once I could grip my ice ax again, we spread out and finished crossing the wall. At that point, and still, to this day, I believe that Lou and Don saved my life.

Years later, when Grace and I lived in the eastern part of the state, we would drive to the Sea-Tac area occasionally, and when we had time, we'd visit Lou while he was in dental school. When I made the trip alone, I'd take my sleeping bag and often slept on Lou's living room floor.

While climbing and hiking or just moving dirt, we'd run into various obstacles and always worked together to overcome them. He, Grace, and I canned peaches together for many summers. We harvested pears and drank beers on more than a few Friday nights. And now again, years later, I was in the Sea-Tac area working late one night, and the car I was driving stalled and would not restart. Finally, I managed to get it off the road, but after trying a couple of times to start the car I gave up.

I decided my best option was to call Lou and talk over my situation. He was a farm boy and understood engines. I was a big-city kid, and all I knew was how to fill the gas tank and turn the starter. And some people will tell you that, until I was in my mid-60s, I wasn't even very good at remembering when to fill up a gas tank. I was notorious for running out of gas.

Within minutes I'd reached him, and he told me just to stay put, and he'd be to me within 20 minutes or so. So he left his family, drove clear across town, got under the hood of my car, pulled a couple of parts, tried a couple of other tricks, and started the car. After the car ran for a few minutes, we both agreed that the car sounded good enough for me to make it home. *And I made it home safely.* Time and time again, we've proved to each other that we are good friends, and over the years, our relationship has grown stronger and stronger.

When we decided to build our own building, we formed what was to become Cotton-Gibson LLC. I decided, and Lou must have, too, that no matter what issues we encountered, we'd be able to work through the issue at hand. With that mindset, we went against legal counsel's advice and split the LLC 50/50. Looking around us over the years and watching many partnerships fail, we both realize that we have been extremely fortunate.

I believe a 50/50 split is dangerous and should be avoided. But Lou and I each had a well-established moral compass, and, luckily, we were and *are* successful.

Creation of the Cotton-Gibson Building

I had started looking for some space for a dental office in the greater Seattle area. In those days, few landlords were willing to lease to dentists. The smell emitted from dental offices wasn't pleasant, and having a dentist in your building limited the types of other tenants willing to lease in the building. After several full days of trying, I made a report to Lou. We are both pretty reasonable problem-solvers, and one of us decided maybe Lou should have his own building. Shortly after that, I found one for him. It was a beautiful building and just about the right size, if not a little too large. Too large is much better than too small. We negotiated a purchase and started the process of buying and figuring out how to redesign the interior as a dental office.

Lou had brought along another dentist who was interested and had looked at a couple of buildings with us. When we started figuring out how to make this newest adventure work, the "other" dentist proposed to Lou that the two of them just dump me and proceed on their own. Lou decided instead to dump the "other" dentist.

It was truly a beautiful building. We were purchasing from a wood products company that was going out of business. They had built the building and used many types of beautiful wood to construct it. After a couple of weeks of hard work, Lou and I realized that to make the building pay for itself, we needed to lease out the second floor. So I dutifully went to the City and asked what we would need to do to be able to lease out the second floor.

To our shock, the answer was "put in an elevator." Now, in those days, retrofitting a building to put in an elevator wasn't as easy as it is today. Retrofitting the building was financially out of our ability, so we had no choice but to walk away from the purchase. To this day, I wish we had figured out some way to purchase and lease out the whole building to some other entity. It was so very nice. That said, we had business to do and needed to figure out how to get Lou more space.

New Opportunities for Cotton-Gibson

One day, several months later, I received a call from Lou. He had taken an unusual way home from work and had seen a lot for sale. He asked if I thought we could have our own building constructed. I said to him, "Sure, let's look into the idea."

Shortly after, we met with the real estate agent handling the sale. Lou and I thought the lot was reasonably priced, and the seller seemed to want to sell, so I started doing some pencil work. Eventually, Grace and I sold something, probably one of the vacant lots, and then did a 1031-real-estate exchange to purchase the lot where Lou and I wanted to build.

As we signed the earnest money agreement, the seller's in-house representative said, "If you two pull this off, I will guide you up Mt. Rainier!"

Lou and I had climbed several mountains together, and we both wanted to climb Mt. Rainier, so that was an added incentive to make our planned building a reality. In fact, at a couple of junctures, it was the only thing that kept me going.

As we worked through the process of buying, we learned a great deal. First of all, our main issue was going to be parking. I tried everything I could think of to identify parking for staff and patients. Next, we needed to find a person to develop the property.

We found parking, but unfortunately, a couple of easements were in the way. The seller eventually provided parking with a little cooperation from one of the entities holding one of the easements. The seller leased us a good-sized portion of a parking lot they owned just east of our proposed building. The seller and its landlord consented to give us "parking rights." That was an interesting process, and I needed to deal with people in several different states to get that all negotiated and finalized.

The other easement was a different kind of problem. One of the major real estate players in the greater Seattle-Tacoma area owned a building to the south at a lower elevation from our proposed building. He had an easement that allowed him to build a ramp to his building should the railroad block his current entrance to his building at any time in the future. His ramp would effectively eliminate the parking on our lot. We weighed our options and finally decided that laying railroad tracks in this day and age is expensive. So, Lou and I took a flier, a major leap in faith, and signed that we understood the easement paperwork, and we continued forward.

Finding a Developer for Cotton-Gibson

The next step: find a developer. We interviewed three developers during a succession of Lou's lunch hours. After the third interview and while on the way back to Lou's office, Lou turns to me and says, "I want you to develop the building."

I said, "Who, me?" Over the next couple of evenings, he explained to me his rationale. First, all the developers we had interviewed wanted a 3 to 6 percent commission on every dollar spent on construction. I had experience running a calculator when I was a State of Washington economist and during my time as a budget analyst. Furthermore, I had experience negotiating contracts when I worked for Indigent Defense and negotiated contracts with defense attorneys. And finally, I liked saving money more than I liked spending it. After a week of discussing the idea with Grace, I told Lou that he and I needed to pick a backup developer just in case I failed, and only then would I agree to try to develop the building. And so, we started.

Finding an Architect, David Weston

Lou and I decided the next thing we needed to do was to find an architect. Lou and I jointly interviewed at least three. The last person we interviewed was David Weston, owner of Commercial Design Associates. How we got to him, I cannot remember. I do remember sitting in his reception room and thinking, "This guy understands money." When we met David, Lou and I were both impressed. We were most impressed with his experience, attitude, business approach, and plan. There was no contest; we hired David.

David proved to be a great hire. He was with us throughout the project and did a terrific job. He reviewed the site, drew a site map, avoided the known easement, and drew us a 70-foot by 100-foot building with two floors, equaling 14,000 square feet of leasable space. And then, when we found another easement, a fire-water easement that wasn't recorded, he cut off the northwest corner of the building, made a great sign location on a busy street, and we ended up with 13,970 square feet. It was to be a two-story, structural brick building. And, with a little hard work, it ended up being a very pretty building and an extremely efficient one. We had won big.

CHAPTER 16

We Bought "The Farm"

One evening, while I was doing paperwork and working the numbers, Grace came into my office visibly upset. I told her to have a seat on my knee and tell me what was wrong.

As it turned out, she had received a call from the younger of her two brothers. There were eight siblings in her family, six girls and two boys. Grace was the third child, one of the "three older kids." Grace's younger brother had inherited the family farm with the formal understanding that he'd take care of their mother until she died.

Grace's mother, who, along with her husband, had always been great to me, had died six months or so before this call.

The facts that came out during the conversation were that Grace's brother had taken a previously free and clear farm and not done well, and the farm was now at risk. Grace's brother offered to sell us the farm if we'd take over the debt. We had 30 days to react, or the bank would foreclose on the property.

What a mess! We didn't have any ready cash to bail out the farm. Grace's brother was a very nice guy, but he just had too many ideas and allowed his debts to keep growing, and eventually, they got out of control.

Grace said she could not stand to have her father's name sullied with having the farm repossessed. "Could you please figure out a way to purchase the farm?"

With interest rates low, we had been receiving offers for 0-percent-interest-rate credit cards. Over the next couple of weeks, we applied for and received seven of the cards with more than $200,000 credit available on them. It was money ready to spend, and in those days, there were not any of the now common cash advance fees.

Five days before foreclosure was scheduled, I showed up outside Louisville, KY, with over $190,000 in our checking account; I wrote out a check and closed on the farm. The farm was now free and clear, and Grace and I now owned it.

While in Kentucky, I applied for a loan at a local bank. *Somehow* the bank took almost eleven months to process the loan. Later, I found out that the bank's branch manager was one of the people who hoped to purchase the farm at foreclosure. We eventually got the loan, and used it to pay off the credit cards before we accumulated interest on any of them.

The Neighbors

Now that we had our building plans together, it was time to apply for the needed permits to build. When we went to the City for permits, we were told we would need approval from the Neighborhood Committee. I quickly found the chairperson of the Neighborhood Committee and arranged to make a presentation at the committee's next meeting.

I made a presentation at the next meeting as an added agenda item. I had David's drawing of the building and the elevations, told the members the target tenants were medical and dental practitioners, and whatever else I could think of that might matter to the neighbors.

I was dismissed after being told the group would discuss the possibilities of allowing the development and that I should return for the next meeting.

Our first delay, I thought.

The next meeting didn't start out a whole lot better than the first. I was asked some questions. I could see some people were not impressed with what I thought was a beautiful building. Finally, someone asked, "What else might the lot be used for? Could it be used as a park?"

During the weeks between the meetings, I had actually received calls from a fast food chain interested in the lot and a porn-shop owner looking to rent space in the building. So I told the Neighborhood Committee that those were two probable outcomes for the vacant lot. After a few more questions, I was told that I'd probably get an answer in the next couple of days.

The next evening, the chairperson called and told me the committee would put their full support behind our building, our development.

What Makes for a Beautiful Building?

Somewhat early in this process, Lou suggested that he and I have breakfast with a guy he knew who had been quite successful as a landlord. The guy purchased, remodeled, and then leased out older homes in an area that was now starting to be viewed as quite attractive since it was "close-in." Always willing to learn, I readily agreed. We met Lou's friend at a local restaurant and sat down for breakfast.

He was eating oatmeal; I saw that as a good sign. I felt that it meant he was both taking care of himself and wasn't a spendthrift. We started by talking about the difficulties of developing real estate. It became clear that the guy was smart—really smart. He had started purchasing single-family dwellings in a poor area close to downtown just after the 1980 crash. He had designed some windows to make them easy to install in those old houses. He'd purchase a house for $10,000 to $15,000; then, he would go into the house, clean it up, and install some windows to brighten the inside. He'd also do some landscaping and then rent the house out. The rental income would most likely pay for all the costs in the first year of operation. I calculated that the first houses were probably free and clear by the end of year four. *Amazing.*

Now, when we were meeting, I decided most of the houses had to be worth $90,000 to $130,000—what a great return on investment. And, what fantastic cash flow!

He told us two items of real importance. Two concepts. One, try to hit a home run on your first building. After that, you can hit singles, doubles, and triples, but regardless of what you are hitting, your home run will carry you unless you totally lose track of the numbers. And two, he asked if we knew the definition of a "Beautiful Building." We both took the hook and said, "No."

He said, "A beautiful building is one that pays for itself." Words of wisdom and experience. That gave us a framework. I think of those two concepts often.

Kurt Kelly and Kelly and Kelly

Next, we needed to find a contractor to actually construct the building. I am not "handy" at all. Also, at the time, I didn't have the contacts or the knowledge to coordinate construction on my own. Even now, having both the contacts and the knowledge, I am not sure I would take on coordinating the construction of an entire building.

So I went out for bids. All four companies we received bids from had good reputations and reasonable bids. I had included a good acquaintance's construction company. One of the principals of the company was Kurt Kelly. Today I am not sure exactly why I asked them to bid, but I did. I was good friends with Kurt Kelly's wife, Julie, as she and I had worked on church committees together, but I didn't know much of Kurt other than his kids said he worked a lot, and Julie said he owned part of a construction company.

At one point, I was talking with Kurt about the job at hand. We were in his conference room when Julie called, and at the end of the conversation, she told Kurt to make sure he gave me a good deal. Pretty quickly, we came to terms, and it was another very good decision for us. Kelly and Kelly was an easy company to work with, they appointed a very experienced construction superintendent to the job, and we ended up with a very good building.

A Very Cold and Windy Morning and Other Adventures

Once we were under construction, more and more questions kept coming our way. Once in a while, a question needed to go to David Weston and CDA, but I made most of the decisions. For some of the really big decisions, I worked with Lou to ferret out an answer.

Lou and I were talking almost every night for anywhere from 20 minutes to two hours. Lou, who passed by the site almost every night, would stop on-site to see what had been accomplished and determine if he had any questions that he thought I should ask the superintendent.

The best story that came out of this system of splitting the work involved the structural brick that was to become the face of the building. The bricks for the design that David Weston had made were ordered. They were shipped via rail and delivered to our construction site. Once the masons took apart the packaging, the owner of the masonry company determined that there weren't enough bricks of one of the colors and too many of the other color. That evening Lou and I spent a long, long evening on the phone. Both of us had small strips of paper in front of us that were the size of little bricks. We kept moving "bricks" and trying to see what "design" we could make that we could like and what designs we didn't like, but all were in the shape allowed and governed by the ratio of the bricks on hand.

The next day, I told the construction super what we had decided. Late that day, the super called to tell me the mason said our design wouldn't work. The mason suggested we meet with him at 5 a.m. the next day, on-site.

I woke up at 3:30 to make the trip. By 5 a.m., Lou, the mason, and I stood by while the mason's employees stacked brick so we could see how different designs would look. The building site was on the top edge of a deep canyon. The canyon runs east and west. The wind was blowing through the canyon and the late winter cold coupled with the wind made for an extremely cold morning. And here was the mason without gloves, stacking and restacking bricks.

Eventually, we found a design that Lou and I liked, and the mason believed feasible. At that point, the mason and his employee stacked more bricks so we could see how a larger section of the building would appear. All three of us still liked the design. And to this day, almost every time I drive by the building, I look at what a nice-looking building we have, and I remember standing in the freezing wind making the design decision. Fun memories.

CHAPTER 17

Tenants Needed

As soon as I knew we would be able to break ground on the building, I started looking for tenants. Lou was going to take some 3,400 square feet, but the rest of the building was vacant and in need of tenants. Pretty quickly, Lou found a young dentist who wanted to relocate from the west side of town, potentially into our building. Relocating across town and across the river wasn't an easy decision for her and included some big risks, but she wanted to consider the idea. A big plus for us was that her husband was an architect. He designed large projects like high schools. They both liked the building, and she eventually signed a lease.

A couple of years later, I found out that she had lost only three patients in making the move. It had been a gutsy move on her part, and it worked; I was relieved. At this point, we still had some 8,200 square feet of vacant space and needed more tenants to get financing for the building.

The Anchor Tenant and a Much-Needed Loan

We had constructed the building using 0-percent credit card debt, just as it had worked out when Grace and I purchased the farm with credit cards at 0 percent for the first year. The construction was to take 90 days, and the credit cards were at 0 percent for 120 days, so I figured things would work out.

Well, we were into the project for over 100 days, and we still didn't have enough space leased to qualify for the loan we had chosen for permanent financing for the building. Then, Jane Bridger decided to bring Western Renal Services, or WRS, to review the building. WRS provides dialysis services, and they were interested. We were too, much more than they would ever know.

WRS wanted a rent rate that would be a lot less than we needed to get the building financed. We countered. Days went by; we were on day 110. I was getting concerned, really concerned.

I was in the Sea-Tac area to check on the building and the existing tenant improvements and to meet with Lou after his work day. Lou came by the building, and as we walked around our new building, I told Lou how scared I was and how I was becoming increasingly concerned about all the credit card debt. One after another, starting soon, all were going to be between 18 and 21 percent.

Ever the calm dentist, Lou said to me, "Just watch; it will all work out."

I thought, *Easy for him to say.* I owed the credit card companies the money. In retrospect, it's funny, but at the time, quite stressful. Relief came when, on day 113, WRS signed a 10-year lease. Once we had the lease in hand, I went directly to the bank, and we closed with permanent financing on day 118. And at that point, the Cotton-Gibson building became a

"Beautiful Building." We didn't know it then, but we do now; we had hit a home run.

Several months later, a pediatric dentist took the last twelve hundred square feet in the building, and our building was 100 percent leased, long term. Lou and I, both being rather conservative when it comes to money, with Grace and Charlotte's consent, started sending every available extra dollar to the bank to pay off the Beautiful Building. We paid it off quite a few years early and have been enjoying the cash flow ever since. It was quite an accomplishment for the two of us and often comes up in conversation.

College for Shirley

About the time we finished the Cotton-Gibson building, it was time for our firstborn, Shirley, to head off to college. This soon-to-occur event led to lots of opportunities. Our family had always enjoyed road trips, so we took Shirley to colleges all over the country. We, as it turned out, *erroneously* assumed every college would want someone like her.

We had our incredible daughter out touring. She had been the student body president with a 4.0 GPA all the way through high school and was valedictorian. She was competitive, having qualified for the district track meet in both her junior and senior years, and had won awards and trips due to her programming skills. She was able to get interviews at both Harvard and Notre Dame. She toured Yale and Pepperdine. We stopped at both UCLA and USC. Thank goodness we all enjoyed all the touring. Ultimately, Washington State was the only school to actively court Shirley.

We did lots of things for the other two kids while making these road trips. At one point, we were in the main Harvard library looking at books that were printed hundreds of years ago. Sam, our middle kid, piped up and said, "Dad, this is great. I'm loving these books. Do you think they'd let us bring our sleeping bags in here for the night so we could read all night?"

Sorry, son!

At Washington State, we all were able to view some letters written by one of the priests who came to the northwest in the late 1700s to convert the Native Americans. The letters were written in French, and we didn't understand any of them, but we did get to see them.

At another university, we were told that if we'd have called ahead, we could have seen an original Louisa May Alcott draft of one of her great books. Marilyn, our youngest, was almost as sad as her mother that we missed that opportunity. But we had fantastic trips.

Eventually, Washington State University courted and recruited Shirley, and she chose to go there. Four years later, she graduated from engineering school as a software engineer. She was immediately picked up by one of the big three, and she progressed rapidly. While at Washington State, she had actually earned enough scholarships and worked enough jobs while in college that she didn't have any school debt when she graduated. Lucky parents—and a wise and thrifty daughter.

And we ended up being lucky parents twice more. More on that later.

The Second Million

Much to our shock, at this point, we calculated that we were worth two million dollars net, if we liquidated everything. The second million, when compared to the first, had been so much easier. Additionally, everyone in the family seemed to be in an enjoyable space, so we decided just to manage everything.

Mark's Idea

Mark Jersey, the owner of JJ-MD Construction, had made Lou's tenant improvements in the Cotton-Gibson building. Lou and I both liked Mark. His company specialized in medical and dental tenant improvements. Lou and I had interviewed him when we were looking for the general contractor for the building. We didn't choose JJ-MD because we were concerned he didn't have enough experience to take on such a large (to us) project. Lou did eventually hire JJ-MD for his tenant improvements, and Mark's crew performed very well.

A few months after the Cotton-Gibson building was completed, Mark called me and suggested we have lunch. A week later, we were having lunch when Mark said we should build some more buildings like the Cotton-Gibson building. He said, "We could offer doctors and dentists an ownership position when they lease space in the buildings." It would be similar to the model Lou and I had been able to put together. We discussed the idea, I promised to work on the numbers, and I suggested that we could use David Weston as the architect. Mark readily agreed with having David be the architect as they had worked together on previous projects. After lunch, we parted and agreed to a future meeting.

The Birth of Equity 4 U LLC

After considering Mark's idea, I had some thinking to do. *How could the idea work? What would implementation look like? What business format should we use?*

Eventually, I decided that we should be formed as an LLC. It is, in my opinion, the easiest type of business to establish, and it provides both protection and, in those days, it could morph as needed.

I felt we would need more than three members. *What/who would be the "right" type of members and the right number?* I decided that we should have five members. Five provides for an uneven number for voting and a wide base of knowledge so that we wouldn't get too focused and not look outside ourselves for information.

Who should be members? I felt Dr. Cotton would be a good member because he was so well-known and connected in the dental sector, and he could probably help us get tenants. Thinking of what else might help, I decided Darryl Houck, my army roommate, could help since he was a CPA and could track the numbers for us.

How to decide on the percentage of ownership and membership in the LLC? I did lots of reading in order to make a suggestion on this issue. I read about the value of a contractor (Mark) and the value of an architect (David). I knew from previous interviews what developers charged (me). I also considered what Lou and I learned in doing the Cotton-Gibson building, especially leasing. Eventually, I took my suggestions and calculations to the group, and we decided.

We discussed the suggestions, everyone asked questions and offered insight, and then we modified the ownership/membership and approved the agreed-upon percentages. We were a real business.

As it turned out, Mark was the smartest of us all in that he took 50 percent of his value in cash, which covered his real costs/outlay, and 50 percent in membership which gave him some of what we all hoped would be long-term value.

We met each week in David's office and made decisions as we went through the process. Darryl was involved via conference call. David did some conceptualization of what one of our buildings might look like. Mark did some basic calculations on the cost of construction. Lou started talking with dentists, and Darryl set up the accounting. We each threw $2,500 into a bucket and decided to make something happen. We had $12,500, and I had time. So, I was told to go out and find land for our first project.

CHAPTER 18

Conventions and a Phone Call

Thinking we had the living end of ideas, we started marketing the idea of Equity 4 U LLC. We made presentations to landowners who might want to become partners by donating their land, and we attended dental conventions. The conventions I remember were Arizona, Oregon, and, of course, Washington. No takers anywhere despite our earnest effort. Then, one day, Lou got a call from a dentist he had known for a while. Karl Vicson, a dentist in a nearby town, heard of our plan and was interested in being a part owner of a building.

I talked with Dr. Vicson, and he was quite interested, so I put together a lease for him that was subject to our ability to deliver a building in a timely manner based on his current lease expiration date. Then, on an area map, I drew a circle representing his patient base. That focused my search for land, and I started looking for a buildable lot.

A Parcel of Land

During the following weeks, I drove every commercial street within the circle. I was looking in and around Renton, WA. I found four parcels of land in the circle that were currently on the market. Eventually, I discovered that Shogun Inc controlled all four lots. I focused on a property on southwest Kirby Drive. I submitted an offer on behalf of Equity 4 U LLC (E4U). Based on David Weston's recommendation, I offered a very competitive price and sought one acre of the parcel. Days of negotiations went by.

Eventually, Paul Shogun, the seller, and I met and discussed what each of us was trying to do. The land had been part of his parent's estate and had been in his family's hands since the early 1920s. He wanted to sell and move to Hawaii. I wanted an office building. He didn't want to deal with multiple people. David Weston and I talked, looked at the properties, and talked again. Eventually, Paul Shogun, his real estate agent, and I devised a four-phase closing plan based on David Weston's drawing and Mark Jersey's schedule.

The Four-Phase Purchase Plan

The first closing would allow E4U to purchase and build the "Karl Vicson" building. The second phase would allow E4U to build on the largest lot. It was large enough for two additional buildings and a two-story parking facility. The third phase would allow for a building, and so would the fourth. We closed on the first lot in November or December 2000.

We were just five guys, our heads down, focused on making something happen. We signed up for all four lots because we believed in our concept and plan. Maybe we were just *crazy*. No matter, obviously, all five of us thought we could do it.

The County

Closing on Phase 1 was contingent on the County approving David Weston's plan. Getting the County's approval at the time seemed a horrible struggle with multiple meetings and many trips from wherever I might be to the County seat. It was a horrible, often very disruptive process.

We were under the gun to get the building completed in time for Dr. Vicson to move into the building, and, at the same time, Lou and I had to find more tenants in order to make the building, 22,500 square feet of space and three stories tall, in a position to qualify for a bank loan.

The one experience I will never forget, as long as I have a memory, is when David Weston told me that the County was ready to issue the permit and that I needed to go purchase it. I took the long drive, checked in at the planning office, and, five minutes or so later, the planner came out from an office and charged at me, yelling loudly, demanding to know why I was there, telling me to leave the building and never come back until the planner called me to come in. It was a horrible scene.

Everyone in the waiting room looked horrified as the planner charged at me and got in my face, yelling and pointing toward the door; even though I did explain why I was there, I could not get the planner to hear me. Not knowing what else to do, I left the building and called David to report. He didn't understand what was going on but would make some inquiries. I was too busy to care and just went back to prospecting for tenants.

The fact is, I never did find out what the communication problem was. I did come to believe that sometimes it isn't worth taking time to know what causes a problem, but instead of thinking about it, it is best to keep working on the *real issues* at hand. So we all just kept working on issues as they came up.

Financing Phase 1

In addition to working to find tenants, I also needed to find financing for Phase 1. Grace and I belonged to a 25-family swimming club. Five families got together some 30 years earlier, bought two city housing lots, and literally built the pool themselves. The contractor dug the hole, the doctors tied the rebar, and the engineer figured out the filter and heating system. Eventually, the organization expanded to 25 families. We were fortunate that the year after we arrived, one of the families was ready to sell their share of the organization, and Grace and I (and family) were allowed to purchase the share.

One of the members was the CEO of a small rural hospital east of town. He was following my project, every twist, and turn. One Saturday, he and I were talking about the project and my need for financing. He told me that the local bank where he worked was expanding and ready to make loans. Monday morning, I called the manager, Steve Waverly, and presented our plan. Shortly after, I started the loan process with that bank. Steve was great to work with, and we eventually received construction financing for Phase 1. At about the same time, we also received a building permit for Phase 1. Mark and crew started construction, and now we needed, *really needed*, more tenants.

Tenant Prospects

By the time we received our building permit and had financing ready, I had four pretty good tenant prospects. They were better than suspects ; they were real prospects. The prospects were a general dentist, an oral surgeon, an endodontist, and a periodontist. I actually had six, but two were recently graduated periodontists, both wanting exclusivity in the building.

I was spending hours each day answering questions and making phone calls. Additionally, every Friday afternoon, at about 3 p.m., I would knock on Dr. Jonathan Snell's office window and encourage him to consider our Phase-1 building.

Dr. Snell, an extremely well-respected oral surgeon throughout much of the state, needed to move his practice but had another building under consideration. Finally, after 10 to 12, maybe even 16, weeks of knocking on his window every Friday afternoon, he told me to "send a draft lease."

The next Friday, lease in hand, I visited; we edited, and then a week later, after dealing with his attorney, Greg Englisher, who had also been Lou Cotton's attorney, we signed a lease. At about the same time, I was working with an endodontist, Dr. David King, who's CPA had questions. The CPA's first question: "How does the E4U Plan work?"

The E4U Plan

The E4U Plan was to offer tenant prospects a portion of the building's ownership, a membership in the LLC that owned the building, in exchange for the tenant signing a 10-year lease and making all of their own tenant improvements rather than E4U having to give them a tenant improvement allowance. The tenant's membership would be equal to one-half of their usable square footage divided by the total square footage of the building. Based on my experience, we believed that we could save on real estate commissions by my doing much of the leasing.

The plan made it so that we could count part of the tenant's improvements as part of the down payment. With David "donating" his commission and Mark donating one-half of his profit, we had, on paper, a pretty good down payment. In the end, some of it worked all the time, and some of it, only some of the time. Most of our early tenants bought into the building, and most came without a real estate commission.

Dr. King's CPA suggested he not buy in and only be a tenant. I didn't feel that was a very good decision at the time, and I am still saddened by it, even today. But, unfortunately, I needed *any* type of tenant we could get, so I could sign another lease. And he, too, came to us without a real estate commission.

Initially, I thought we could do around 3,000 buildings . The numbers worked, and I thought the bankers would be satisfied with them. I had dreams. As it turned out, the E4U Plan produced seven buildings worth somewhere around 64 million dollars today, 2018. Not what we expected or hoped for, but nothing to laugh about.

The $64 million is what E4U and affiliates put together.

CHAPTER 19

Elevation, Elevation

The second parcel E4U was going to purchase wasn't easy, topographically. It was situated with Stewart Road to the north and Kirby Drive to the south. There was a medical building to the east, higher up on the hillside than our site, and down at the bottom of the hillside was a storage complex, and below that, some wetlands.

Paul Shogun, the seller, told me his family once lived on the second lot. He had stories of hauling water from the family's wetlands all the way up the hillside for use in the house, which had been located in the southeast portion and the highest part of the hillside. He described it as a long, arduous slog, and it sure looked like it would be one to me. According to David Weston, the elevation gain from the west to the east was over 70 feet. I pictured it while writing this, and I think it could easily be considered over 85-90 feet, but David is the professional, so I will take his word on the subject.

David's Drawings

In David's words, "The topography, though overwhelming for some, provided unique opportunities to create a two-building-plus parking facility campus without having to move an overwhelming amount of dirt." So David designed a professional campus with two buildings and a parking facility in the middle. It was ingenious.

The Building

The Phase-1 purchase, and the easiest building site to develop, was in the southwest part of town. David Weston had designed a three-story, 22,500-square-foot building. The floor plan was 75 by 100 feet for a total of 7,500 square feet per floor. Parking for the building was to be to the north of the building. For financing purposes, we needed more than four parking spots per every 1,000 square feet of usable office space. Starting with a plan that had a large foyer and wide hallways limited our initial parking requirement.

To start construction, we needed to show we could produce 72 parking spaces. David outlined the parking spaces, and the seller allowed for a little overlap into areas we were to purchase in the future.

The day after we received approval from the bank, Mark and one of his supervisors started the earth-moving. As the days went by, either Mark, David, or I was on-site virtually every day. I was almost always in the area prospecting for new tenants. We put out signs on southwest Stewart Road and started getting inquiries. Finally, we had officially started and had construction financing, a lot more money than our original $12,500.

Building 1, the Jersey Building

The first parcel was nice and level. Mark's crew started construction. And then, the rain started. One day, the construction was moving along, and we were on schedule. The following week, when I checked in, the construction team was slogging through mud over two inches deep. Everything was wet and covered with mud. Mark took immediate action and quite literally saved the day. By 9 p.m., the parcel was covered with straw, and the building's foundation was encapsulated by a large tent, one of the largest I have ever seen.

Darryl Houck Visits

Shortly after we broke ground, Darry Houck flew out from Florida to see what we were doing. Darryl stayed with Grace and me in Tacoma. I picked Darryl up from Sea-Tac, and we drove to Renton so he could see the sites and how they were planned.

I drove him in to look at parcel one. He was pleased to see all the progress. It was late spring, the building was complete, and tenant improvements were well underway.

We then drove to parcel two. I stopped at the southwest corner of the parcel, and we stood there watching dirt move, stakes being pounded into the ground, and we looked at the forms being set up for the first concrete pour. We watched for about a half-hour, and Darryl turned to me and said, "Ron, this project is too big. Someone is going to decide they want more of the project, and you will get in a long fight, probably a legal fight, about the project, and the project will fail. I need out."

I was startled and really upset. That said, knowing Darryl, my wise, long-term friend who dealt with some rather large projects in south Florida, was, for him, right. I could not argue with him, and I feared he might be right. Darryl gave the rest of us a break and left his $2,500 in the project.

A benefit to his visit is that eventually, the two of us were able to get in contact with a long-lost officer-candidate-school friend, Jim East. Darryl, Grace, and I were chatting one evening when Darryl told us that the last time he'd seen Jimmy was just after the two of them had landed in Viet Nam. Upon parting, Jimmy had told Darryl, "If you ever want to get a hold of me, just write "Jim East," Jake, Iowa, and it will get to me."

So, I ran to my office, picked up a pen, paper, envelope, and stamp, and we wrote a note to Jim asking, hoping, for contact.

Several weeks later, I heard from Jimmy. He had gone home to Jake for the weekend, and while walking in downtown Jake on Sunday afternoon, the postmaster stopped him and told him there was a letter waiting for him. We were in contact!

Jimmy, Darryl, and I have done a lot together in the years since. It has been over 20 years now, and we communicate almost monthly and seem to get together every year or so. That was a real silver lining resulting from a real downer moment.

Prospecting for Tenants

Lou and I made call after call, searching for folks who might be interested in being a tenant in our first building. The next doctor to come on board was Dr. Rick Ash. I don't remember who, how, or why Dr. Ash called me, but he did, and he soon signed a lease. Dr. Ash was very influential in the dental community and a welcome addition.

Next came Dr. Kevin Kwee. At the time, Dr. Kwee was a newly-minted general dentist. Like Drs. Vicson, Snell, and Ash, he bought into the building. Dr. King's CPA had advised him only to sign a lease but to take the tenant improvement money we were offering doctors, and by then, that was our only out-of-pocket extra expense.

A few weeks later, we had two newly-minted periodontists looking at the building. Both seemed to have great attitudes and wanted to buy into the building. Eventually, because he was the first to produce a signed lease, we signed up Dr. Robert Henry. And a few weeks later, we were able to sign a lease with an internist, Dr. O'Clarey. That filled the building to capacity. Building 1 would pencil—one down, four to go.

Carolyn Jackson, CPA

With Darryl gone, E4U needed a CPA. While discussing the issue at one of our weekly meetings, David Weston suggested Carolyn Sunrise. David's company CDA had worked with Carolyn for years, and he thought she was excellent. So Grace and I interviewed Carolyn. Grace and I had experience with a wide range of accountants. Grace knew what she wanted. Some just knew how to do the books but couldn't explain them to us. Others seemed to both know how to do the books and also how to translate them so we could understand them.

Carolyn was and is quite articulate. She had worked in a medium size CPA firm in the Sea-Tac area. It was actually one that I had used at one point in my younger years when I needed help with a tax return. She had started her own company in order to have more control of her life. I really identified with that idea. And she gave us an idea of how she interpreted "the rules." I preferred accountants who pushed the limits a little. On the other hand, accountants who push the rules too far scare me. I always figured that I was aggressive enough that I didn't need someone doing our books who was more aggressive because I didn't need to be audited again.

After talking later that evening with Grace, she and I decided Carolyn would be great. As it turned out, Carolyn would end up doing taxes not only for E4U and all of its buildings, but also for our entire family. Carolyn also does the books for all the companies Grace and I are involved in and the companies I have acquired on my own in more recent years. Carolyn is terrific! We feel very fortunate to work with her.

Of course, when we see our tax returns that pile almost two feet high, we wonder what in heaven's name we have done. Starting three years ago, in 2015, we got our returns electronically. Grace keeps them all and keeps the banks happy. The returns and reporting would really almost be too much for me. I'm fortunate.

CHAPTER 20

College for Sam

Amid all the construction and day-to-day pandemonium, Sam graduated from high school and was ready to go off to college. Sam did well in high school. His sister, Shirley, had been student body president, valedictorian, and person of the year, and Sam held his own place too. The school had three top awards for students: person of the year, girl of the year, and boy of the year. Grace and my kids were never part of the "in-crowd." We had tried to bring them up as individuals, independent and able to chart their own paths. So we were amazed when Shirley became person of the year.

This time around, with Sam, who didn't keep us up to date as much as Shirley had, we were shocked and delighted as Sam was announced as boy of the year!

Central High wasn't a gigantic school, but it was a reasonable size, with just over 2,000 students—500 plus per class.

Sam was such an individual. Even though he was almost 6'5", he did not enjoy athletics. He was present enough that he stood up to some of the football players and ended up with a number of good friends in that group, and held his own in weight-training class. Sam had been student body secretary for his junior and senior years. He'd held the position because he ran a great campaign his sophomore year, in large part, for two reasons. First, Grace encouraged him to use a campaign photo of himself at about age seven, and second, Sam decided to use a happy face as his logo for the campaign. His classmates and schoolmates must have liked his campaign.

He stayed as student body secretary for a second year, mainly because two others, both young women, decided they wanted to be student body president and vice-president, and Sam couldn't see any reason to rock the boat or buck "the system." Funny kid, good decisions.

Unlike Shirley, Sam didn't have any interest in looking around at schools. He told me, "Dad, Washington State has a good program and really great food; why would I go anyplace else?"

How could I fight such logic? As things worked out, Sam received an ROTC scholarship, a full ride for college if he finished in the engineering school, and he was off to school in a flash. Like Shirley, he chose to be a resident assistant in a dormitory, and between his RA work and his ROTC scholarship, he could get through school without debt. Lucky parents and another wise and thrifty kid.

Mark Jersey's Wall

It was time to start setting up Phase 2 on parcel two by then. Mark and his company needed to start work on the west wall to allow us to level the lot and hold up part of the parking lots. It was going to be mammoth. It would be almost two hundred feet long and reach almost forty feet in height at some points.

The earth started moving, and then the rain came. One day, I watched the workers slog through the mud and wondered how they could do their job under such conditions. The south end of the wall went up first. George Sanderson, who engineered the wall, was on-site periodically, assuring us that the wall was well-designed. Throughout the wall's history, George has been a calming influence.

As work continued, it became more and more obvious how large the wall was going to be. Incredible. One day, David Weston and I were watching the work on the wall, and David turned to me and said, "This is the closest you will ever come to feeling like a king."

Mark Jersey brings FS-NW

Just after construction started on the west wall of parcel two, Mark came to a meeting and told us that the Fracture Specialists - Northwest (FS-NW) was looking for a new home. FS-NW was a reasonably-sized office and surgery center. Reasonable to the real world, gigantic to us.

The very next day, I started talking with Anita Bolsinger, the administrator of FS-NW. Anita outlined what she and the doctors wanted. I told her I thought we could deliver, and I immediately drove over to David's office and asked if we could.

He reviewed the plan for the parcel and determined that we could combine the two buildings, thereby giving FS-NW what the doctors and Anita wanted: 16,000+ square feet on one floor. David and I met with Anita, showed her the plan, and told her that we would need the County's permission to change the plan. The revised plan called for the two buildings to move together and for the parking facility to move to the north end of the property. In addition, the wall, which was still under construction, would need to be extended another fifty feet. We explained to Anita that we needed a lease in order to start that process; after all, it was going to cost some real dollars. So, we drafted the lease to be contingent on our ability to obtain the County's permission to change the site plan. Anita went to her board for approval.

Within a week, we had a lease. David worked out the architectural details and went to the County. Mark's team started laying the groundwork for the new combined building and the parking facility. Money was getting tighter and tighter.

MIRATT and the Luck Factor

At about the same time, I figured out E4U needed some real money, and soon. Even though FS-NW expanded its lease to cover two complete floors of the two buildings, we still needed to somehow pay for the parking facility.

Looking ahead, we knew we had to complete the wall, prep the site for the second and third combined buildings, and prepare to start the parking facility. The numbers were scary, and if people didn't continue to buy in, we were going into a very deep hole.

There weren't going to be any tenants on the wall or in the parking facility, so our sweat equity approach wasn't going to work to cover enough of the cost of those features.

And then FS-NW decided not to buy in.

Now, during what appeared to be the period of our greatest need, I received a call about a possible investor in our project.

As it turned out, MRATT of Seattle had sold a property and wanted to do a 1031-tax-free exchange into another property. We were a prospect to be their 1031-exchange target property. MRATT was a group of three CPAs. MRATT stands for "Money Right Again This Time." Nice guys.

A short time later, I met with them. They were interested in what we were doing, but we had one snag. Eventually, we had to meet with three or four people from the real estate group that referred MRATT to us, which also, luckily, represented the CPA's accounting business's lease in their current building.

The seven or eight of us sat in a room discussing what was to be purchased and how. The real estate agents wanted the sale price to be based on everything completed to date, plus the four buildings planned. I pitched that the best decision for the project would be the vacant lot destined for the combined buildings with a parking facility. At some point, the CPAs spoke up and said they had decided they wanted to exchange into the vacant lot destined for the combined buildings.

The deal's outcome ended up being a much smaller exchange, total price, than the newest agent in the room expected. After things calmed down, I figured out that he had expected a much larger purchase and, therefore, a much larger commission. Sadly, for me, too, he was the person who happened to bring me the most optimum and timely deal.

The senior real estate agents, understanding the importance of keeping all relationships in good order, ushered the new member of their firm out the door, promising better times ahead for him.

For a while, I sat with the MRATT CPAs, John, Frank, and Doug, as we discussed how we would move forward.

To this day, I do not know who or what entity paid the real estate commissions, if any. I do not remember seeing an invoice.

At the end of the day, the E4U LLC ended up with almost $450,000 in cash, all of which went into Phase 2 and its great wall and parking facility, which, most importantly, included the purchase of the lot.

We looked good to go.

CHAPTER 21

Back to the County

During our development, the County had the reputation of being quite difficult. And, from my standpoint, once again, they were difficult. We were not moving either of the two buildings very far; we were just raising one, lowering the other, and moving them closer together. To their credit, I believe the County was concerned about extending the wall and ensuring the parking facility had a solid foundation. After spending yet another $20,000 for permits and taking a few weeks off the construction schedule, we finally obtained approval to combine the buildings.

Combining the buildings came with one significant condition laid on us by the County. We could not combine the buildings at the ground floor as we needed to keep the two building footprints in place and build the connection off the ground so that people could walk from one side of the campus to the other. Not just from one side to the other side but from one street to the other, Western Drive to Stewart Road. We complied and were able to get the buildings constructed in time for FS-NW to move.

But, think about this, it rains and rains and rains in the Renton area. How many people are going to want to walk 300 yards in the rain? *Three hundred yards!* Looking back through the years, there have been a few people who ride the bus to campus, but there has been very little use of the street-to-street walking path. I suggest to you that, at most, no more than a half-dozen people a year make that trek across that very valuable space. That said, it wasn't worth a fight. The focus was and had to be on getting the two buildings combined and up. And we were able to make that target.

Financing for the Combined Buildings

Financing for Phase 2 was pretty easy. We had a big-name tenant that had taken 16,000 square feet, and they had verbally agreed to take another 16,000 square feet. Furthermore, we had a real money down payment and a track record. Phase 1, was completed, and, most importantly, it was paying for itself. I went to Western States Bank in downtown Seattle, applied, and got a loan for the combined buildings.

At about this same time, I was able to get permanent financing for Phase 1.

Building 3

The focus on combining the two buildings paid off as we were able to construct the combined building, and we got the tenant. Eventually, FS-NW would lease over 43,000 square feet of the 48,000 square foot leasable space in the combined buildings.

The rest of the story is that the doctors decided not to buy into the building because three of the doctors were about ready to retire, and three were new doctors with lots of student loans.

Even though the three doctors in the middle of their careers wanted to buy in, they were outvoted 6 to 3.

Our newfound money worked, but only because we gave FS-NW a very good lease rate and, therefore, only needed to give them a few dollars for tenant improvements.

It was another win/win, my favorite type of transaction. And the best part for us was that the building became financeable.

The Wall, Again

JJ-MD's subcontractor for the wall for Phase 2 was Ellington, Inc. Ellington was a large company familiar with moving tons of earth, just the type of company we needed. Ellington was charging us and charging us, and we could not and did not pay. Eventually, a lien notice showed up in our home, the office. Western States bank called and asked, "What's up?"

I contacted the CFO at Ellington and requested a meeting. He and I met. I showed him where our next two bank draws on the financing of Phase 2 would become available, and we negotiated a payment plan. He and I would have several such meetings. Money was extremely tight, and times were tough, but they would get tougher and tougher.

The Phase 3 Lot

Time was running out on the purchase of what had become phases three and four of the purchase plan, the two additional sites we had agreed to purchase. I met with the seller's attorney, who held us up for an additional $25,000, which we could ill afford, but then we agreed that E4U would be able to purchase the fourth lot on a payment plan. This was a tremendous plan, a license to defer. Soon we would need that license. The Phase-4 lot was designed to be E4U's billboard. In retrospect, I could have probably held off and maybe not paid the extra $25,000, but I didn't, and, in the end, the $25,000 was the least of the issues we encountered while developing the rest of the project.

Bill Hayburner to the Rescue

William (Bill) Hayburner and I had been friends for many years. We both sold financial products. I sometimes sold products that Bill had. Bill was still a financial advisor. In the old days, he and I cooperated as we tried to find better products for our customers. E4U was running low on cash, so I presented an investment opportunity to Bill: "Buy into the Phase 2 combined buildings, and I will give you a very good deal."

I needed the money so I could give FS-NW the cash for their tenant improvement, and I thought that Bill would see that the combined buildings were a good bet for his customers. I'm sure it all came together because Bill trusted me. Bill ended up buying in and brought along two of his clients. The three new members of Phase 2 and 3 LLC contributed just over $100,000, and each received 2.26 percent of the building. So we may have given up a lot, but we were saved again.

The three of them ended up with a tremendous deal, but their investment in Phase 2 was quite chancey, and they took quite a risk. When you take risks like that, you deserve a good deal, and they saved the campus.

The Wall Is Falling!!

So I quit that week feeling pretty good. I had enough money to get us to the most crucial point in development. I had told the group repeatedly that the worst possible place for the development to slow or stop would be to have three buildings, the wall, and the parking facility completed and two buildings left to go. We would need at least one more building leased so it can help pay for the last building site.

Monday morning, I headed back to work after having worked on multiple spreadsheets over the weekend. The news wasn't very good, on two fronts. One, the weather had been horrible from a construction standpoint. It had rained torrential rains for five straight days. As a result, I was sure construction had been shut down at the sites. The other was money. Over the weekend, Grace had paid bills, and we barely had enough money to pay for Phase 2 and part of its parking facility.

And then, I arrived at Phase 2. Work had stopped, but a group of people was still standing at the west end of the site looking at the wall. As I walked up, the site superintendent looked up and said to me, "It appears the wall is falling; it is collapsing."

Then, I find out that no one has done anything other than watch our dreams collapse. I called Mark and David and let them know of the issue. I called George Sanderson, talked with him, and he said he would be right over.

About forty-five minutes later, George arrived and started telling the few construction workers still on-site how to relieve the pressure on the wall. A short while later, Mark and David arrived. The four of us met for a few minutes. George told me to order a survey and that we should all meet at his office Wednesday morning to discuss the survey results and look at the path forward.

Wednesday morning, we were all in George's conference room before 7:30 a.m. George had taken some soil samples and had the samples analyzed. He had the data from the survey, and he had drawings to show us. As it turned out, the first excavator Mark had hired had not compacted the soil as required. The excavator had left his abandoned equipment on-site and didn't ever show up for work again. He had just disappeared. When soaked with water, the relatively loose soil weighed too much and stretched the netting holding back the soil, and the bulge in the wall was getting larger and larger.

Monday, the rain had finally become intermittent showers. The construction crew was out taking apart the south end of the wall. Most of the center and north end appeared stable. Ellington did most of that work.

Tuesday, our 22- to 25-foot-high portion of the wall was now about 4 feet high. George stayed on-site to supervise.

Then, rebuilding began and appeared to be successful—quite a scare.

We Have Money and Some Time and Then...

Things were starting to look good again, and it appeared we could get Phase 2 with its parking facility constructed; however, there would still be debt on the soon-to-be-completed wall, Ellington, and the monthly $25,000 payments on the Phase-3 lot. And we still had two more buildings to construct.

Some good news is that we could pay for the wall rebuild over time. That helped a great deal.

Before we ever started the Phase-1 project, I warned everyone multiple times that the worst place for us to be caught flat-footed was when we had the wall, the parking facility, and three buildings constructed. After all, we had committed to purchasing all four lots. If we got stalled then, the project, our projects would likely be doomed.

The fact is, things looked really good, even great, in that we had the entire Phase-1 building leased. We just needed to finish Phase 2, the wall and the parking facility. That looked to be completed in about eight more weeks.

Then one day, out of the blue, Mark suggested we bring in a fifth member and that all the equity for the new member should come out of *my* membership in E4U. That was to include Phase 2 and the rest of Phase 3.

I totally missed the drumbeat. I tried to explain to him that my whole life and a good part of Grace's were being spent on the project; he had his day job.

He then suggested a couple of different people. Our team was falling apart. I was shocked; I didn't know what to do. One of Mark's suggestions was a real estate agent; another was "someone who could help me." I just totally missed that Mark had an issue. I was busy with the purchase of the Phase-3 and Phase-4 lots, leasing space, figuring out financing, and keeping track of money. And, since Darryl Houck left, Grace had been doing the books on each building and for E4U. I was busy, extremely busy. Slammed.

I never understood what Mark was trying to do. Or why. During the first 45–90 days of the "discussion," I thought he was trying to find someone to take a load off my back. Some of the people he suggested sounded like they might be able to help, but several others didn't. *Was he trying to make another business connection for his company?*

Then, when David started suggesting people, I became concerned. I understood why David was taking Mark's side. Their relationship was somewhat symbiotic. They fed each other jobs.

Luckily, Lou knew who I was and trusted me.

CHAPTER 22

A Long Ugly Fight

The fight over the Campus began in earnest about the time we finished Phase 2, November 2003. David Weston sided with Mark Jersey, and Lou Cotton sided with me. We didn't have a fifth member to break up or help facilitate a settlement. It was ugly, and it was ugly. It would end up lasting for almost thirty-four months.

I somewhat understood why David went along with Mark. Mark could give him more business. What I didn't understand was Mark's issue. He had his day job and was receiving significant equity in each building, plus one-half of most contractors' OHP (overhead and profit), for all the work he was doing on campus. It is still a mystery to me today. I am sure it wasn't greed as Darryl Houck had suggested; there was something else. I suspect that Mark just might not have realized how much time I was working on making the campus happen.

I am pretty sure I wasn't complaining; that is not my style, but the work was consuming my life. Whatever it was, it was a very, very difficult thirty-four months.

Meanwhile

In the meantime, as the fight continued, E4U was bleeding money. I was making $3,200 per month on my retirement, and Grace was making $2,400 per month at her half-time job. To keep the project alive, Grace and I started selling off assets.

As the months wore on, we liquidated some small items, including the old pediatric clinic, which a developer paid generously for. Later, Grace figured out we would get more money selling two 12-plexes than we would for one 24-plex. Since the 24-plex was already on two separate lots with twelve units on each lot, we moved forward with the idea.

Then, Carolyn figured out how we could minimize tax on the first sale, so we sold a 12-plex and put all that money into the campus. And the days dragged on and on.

The Long Ugly Fight, Survival

The fight continued. Months went by. Then a year and then two. At some point into the fight, maybe four months, Lou suggested, and we decided, to make an offer to buy out Mark and David.

We came up with a number, gave it to Mark and David, and told them that we would buy or sell at that price. A few weeks later, Mark and David sent us a number. Lou and I said we'd sell. Mark said, no, that number was only if we bought. Considering the new information, Lou and I recalculated and submitted another number and said we would buy or sell at that price. Mark and David would counter again with a one-sided number. Crazy. This went on for months and months, chewing up money in three- and four-month chunks. We went round and round, seven or even eight times, as money kept going up in smoke. Each time, the time-lags kept getting longer.

New Life and Ann Cotton

In early 2005, Mark had a heart attack while playing golf. He was rushed to the hospital and was stabilized. Then in late March, David's wife filed for divorce.

Mark and David decided to take Lou's and my most recent offer on Friday, April 15, 2005. Lou and I were the buyers. Now, April 15th is tax day. Up until this point in my life, I hadn't ever liked April 15th. In fact, I hated it. Now, each year, I celebrate April 15th.

Grace and I could not have lasted much longer. We were running out of easy-to-liquidate assets. Lou's major assets were his dental business and his 401K. Neither of those was liquid. But there was help.

About eight weeks before the settlement, Lou's wife, Ann Cotton, knowing E4U's circumstances were dire, liquidated some stock and bought into Phases 2, 3, and 4. Ann had been a successful occupational therapist but had left her job shortly after Lou's dental practice had become self-supporting. Then, a short while later, Ann had taken over the dental practice's books. She has a lot of talent and is a very smart person. Ann was an investor on the side and often reads the Wall Street Journal.

Grace and I had sold almost everything we owned and even had taken out a second mortgage on our house to make it through the Long Ugly Fight, so E4U needed some real cash quickly. Ann heard of our concerns and decided to invest. She ended up investing in the project three or four times. As it turned out, that would be the last investment we would need to finish the project. So we were definitely back to having four team members, Lou, Grace, Ann, and me. It is a good feeling to have teammates all pulling in the same direction.

We could continue forward.

Weller Trip

Having planned for this day, I had been in contact with Weller Trip, WT, a well-respected construction contractor team in central-western Washington. They knew my situation and that I was awaiting the settlement of the long fight. They also knew that the building permit for Phase 3 would expire on Monday, April 18th.

As soon as Mark and David signed the agreement I had drafted, I left the room and called WT.

Monday morning, April 18th, a WT project superintendent met on-site with a county inspector. The superintendent shoveled some dirt while the inspector watched, and we were officially "under construction." We saved all the building permit fees, tens of thousands of dollars we could ill afford to lose.

Kathy Walks

I then called and told our first-floor tenant, Dr. Walden, that we were under construction.

Dr. Kathy Walden had been a delight to deal with when we negotiated her lease for the first floor of the Phase-4 building, Building A.

Unfortunately for Lou and me, the time for her to be able to finish her tenant improvements expired about 15 days after the long, ugly fight finished. Since tenant improvements take 90 days and we didn't even have a building yet, Kathy needed to walk away from the project. When the deadline arrived, I received a nice letter from her in which she informed us that she would not be able to take the space and requested her earnest money back. It was a sad, scary day for me when I asked Grace to send back Dr. Walden's earnest money. I'd not only miss talking with Dr. Walden, but I'd miss the tenant and the earnest money.

What I felt best about was that Kathy had found a buildable lot a few miles from the Phase-4 building. She ended up constructing her own building, and she was able to move into her new building when her next lease extension expired. That said, Kathy's leaving meant that the Phase-4 building was under construction, and we didn't have a single tenant for the building. *No tenants.* NONE.

A real motivator. No rest for the wicked.

MRATT

At about this time, Fred, part of MRATT LLC, informed me that, according to his calculations, MRATT did not get enough of the portion of the campus they had invested. Fred had his view. I actually thought my numbers were pretty good. After all the struggle I had been through during the previous couple of years with Mark and David, I just wanted everyone happy. MRATT was a great partner. Fred asked that MRATT's membership be increased from 10 to 10.5 percent; I countered with 11 percent. I wanted MRATT to be a part of the team. Lou and I had gone it alone for too long. Needless to say, MRATT agreed, and I needed to pivot and continue focusing my work on making the Phase-3 building viable.

CHAPTER 23

Tenants for the Phase-3 Building

We had the building under construction, and we needed some tenants so we could get construction financing for the building.

Chris Brinkley and one of the fastest growing banks in the region stepped into the breach just before Kathy Walden left. So, just before our first draw request was due, our leased square footage had gone from 7,000 to zero. Not good.

I tried every method I could think of to find tenants: Craigslist, word of mouth, campus signage. Nothing seemed to be working, and then I had an idea. I went to Lou, Bill Hayburner, Steve Snell, and Karl Vicson and asked each of them if they would back up their investment by leasing space in the Phase-4 building. I requested each sign a lease between 1,200 and 1,500 square feet. I also signed a lease on behalf of E4U. I told them that if they ever had to pay on the lease, I would personally make sure they were paid back. And, I meant it, I could always go back to work and pay people off.

That way, if asked, I could say I had some folks who could move into the building when it was completed. They would all honor their leases. They might not be happy, but they were all good for it.

Within days of getting the underlying leases, I had three entities vying for the first floor. Two of them eventually fell to the wayside, one out of fear, the other deciding the location just wasn't right. The third, Dr. Paul Thompson, needed space. He is a pediatrician. He was separating from a joint practice and really liked the building, the timeline, the location, and the opportunity. One day, he called me and said, "Let's do it."

I had a tough day planned, but, of course, he was going to be my priority. After discussing our mutual schedules, we agreed to meet at a popular truck stop halfway between Seattle and Tacoma. He pulled into the lot, and I put the lease on the hood of his car; he signed the lease, we shook hands, and off we went, me back to Tacoma and he back to Seattle. We had our first tenant, and almost two-thirds of the first floor was leased. *Relief.*

Paul Thompson and Others Who Made the Phase-3 Building Work

Dr. Thompson, locally known as Dr. Paul, has a very inspirational story; I've read his book. Eventually, he would take over the entire first floor of Building A, but in the beginning, he took about two-thirds of the first floor, and that was a good start for us.

Next came Dr. Michelle Standing. She was a fresh-out-of-school pediatric dentist. She had a great attitude and a good plan. We devised terms that would allow her to get in, get up and running, and then get caught up on her unpaid rent eventually. From my point of view, this was a bit of a flier, but she had direction, and I could feel it: great attitude, great track record coming out of school with a great plan. Now the question was, can she implement the plan? I was so very confident that she could, I signed her up. Her practice has continually grown to the point now that she has both a pediatric and a teen dentistry practice in the building. She now leases over two-thirds of the second floor.

Next, in quick succession, came Dr. Gerald Richardson and Dr. Amy Judicial. Dr. Richardson took half of the third floor for a sleep clinic. Dr. Judicial, a newly-minted orthodontist, took up space for a small practice on the third floor. Dr. Richardson and Dr. Judicial both bought into the building. Equity 4 U now had another tenant, developer, and investor-owned building. That was the plan, and we felt quite fortunate to be back to it.

And, when Dr. Doug Halen, a prosthodontist, came into the building, Lou, Bill, Steve, and Karl's leases all disappeared. Another building was paying for itself.

Chris Brinkley and Team

We now had to start looking for permanent financing for the Phase-3 building. Western States Bank had again provided the construction financing, but for whatever reason, they did not want the permanent financing. With our new tenants, longer leases, and tenant owners, it was all looking good on paper, and I thought we would be considered a strong property. Enter Chris Brinkley. I think Chris was probably out prospecting when we met. I will tell you that Chris is a very intelligent, motivated, hard worker. Over the next several years, Chris ended up financing or refinancing all of the five buildings. And, I am pretty sure that in the end, Chris knew more about Grace and me and our properties than we did. He was customer service personified. When he and his team first gave us the financing for this building, I was quite pleased. And then, after Chris verified my numbers and validated the leases, the bank he worked for gave us permanent financing for the Phase-2 building. Now, a reasonable comfort zone for E4U as Phases 1, 2, and 3 all had permanent financing.

College for Marilyn

Now our baby was ready to go off to college. Marilyn had heard all of the WSU stories from Shirley and Sam. Almost all of the stories were positive. She had hoped to go to school in Europe but with everything else going on we couldn't afford to take our eyes off of E4U. So, Marilyn consented to attending WSU.

For Grace and me, it was a sad, crying-filled day for us as we dropped Marilyn off on the first day of college. It all went so fast. She was so little and then a college student. After we had moved her in, and as she walked toward her dorm room, all I could see were the guys watching her.

She went on and forged a different path than her siblings. She did not join ROTC. She did not become a resident assistant either. But she knew how to get the most out of a dollar. She figured out long before anyone else I knew, long before it was talked about, that collegiate housing was a big money maker for the universities. She moved off campus as soon as she was allowed to and then did a terrific job of managing her expenses: mostly lodging and meal costs. She, like her mother, figured out the least expensive way to obtain the books for various classes. In the end, she, too, graduated without any debt.

Marilyn just kept exploring opportunities until she discovered real estate on her own. She now owns a couple of rentals and is licensed to sell real estate in both Washington and Oregon. She watches the market carefully to buy, restore and sell homes at a profit and has had great success. We are very proud and lucky parents indeed. And if you want a great real estate agent, get a hold of me because I have an amazing agent for you.

Olympia and Dr. Todd Weddle

At about this time, I received a phone call from Dr. Todd Weddle. Dr. Weddle had heard about what Dr. Cotton and I put together, and Dr. Weddle wanted a building in Olympia, Washington. *Opportunity.*

Olympia looked like it would be another home run similar to the Cotton-Gibson building. Most of the dentists were in old rundown buildings, and there were a lot of doctors in one rundown building just north of town. We located a building lot and purchased it from a regional retailer. Great lot, lots of room, and we were ready to go.

David Weston wasn't available to us any longer, so I chose a nearby architect. The architect eventually designed a two-story, 20,000-square-foot building. Unfortunately, I wasn't watching carefully enough, so the building is not as efficient as one of David's buildings, but it was a very good-looking building.

Shortly after Weller Trip started construction on Phase 3, I asked them to construct Olympia. A few days after construction started on Olympia, I was approached by the same dialysis company we had in the Cotton-Gibson building. We negotiated an agreement on a lease that covered almost 80 percent of the first floor with an option to take the rest of the floor. Once Dr. Weddle signed, we were financeable.

Darryl George, who I had met when he worked on the Phase-3 building, was now going to be the project superintendent for the Olympia building. The building would not be a "home run." In fact, despite our significant efforts, it took a long, long, long time to make it pay for itself. It was more like a bunt single. It was financed at a 7 percent fixed rate for 15 years. For almost its entire run, it would be a poor loan for us. At the time, it looked really good. It had not been fully amortized, so we still owed money on the building when it was due. My decision. My fault. The market changed, and I didn't see it coming.

In coordination with Weller Trip, we were able to keep costs down while the building was under construction. Additionally, in keeping with our E4U concept, we did not charge the building any developing fees. As a result, it was financeable before we needed the financing.

Twelve years after construction was completed, it has taken off and is now making some very good money. A few months ago, the LLC, the Olympia Professional Building, paid off the building. Not bad for a bunt single.

CHAPTER 24

A Vacant Lot and Straw

Another spring was upon us. As we get further into spring in Washington, dry weather often comes to town. Dry weather means dust. Dust in the air is not good for several reasons, not to mention allergies. Laws have even been passed that make owners responsible for preventing dust from spreading from their properties.

There was still one undeveloped lot that E4U had agreed to purchase. We received a notice from King County that I needed to "make the lot environmentally safe" and ensure it wasn't spreading dust. *How* to do that was my question. As I read the circular, I noticed I could just spread straw over the lot. So, that is what I did.

Finding, purchasing, transporting, and spreading straw on a lot is not as easy as it might appear. For me, it was a harrowing experience and a very exhausting couple of days too. Overcasting this exercise was the fact that the economy had slowed down, and I wasn't seeing any tenant prospects. However, the overall project was in pretty good shape now that we had four operational buildings, each paying operating costs and E4U paying for the vacant lot.

After getting the straw job done, I told myself that I just had to plan to do that job every year for at least the next five years, maybe as long as ten years. I didn't look forward to it, but I'd had worse times in my life.

An Excruciating Closing

Just before she started her junior year in college, Marilyn decided she wanted to stop renting and move into something longer-term. She had hoped to purchase a house to build equity as quickly as possible; however, we, her parents, weren't keyed in at this point, and a condo ended up being the mutually agreed-upon best option for her. She contacted us to discuss purchasing the condo, and Grace and I both supported the idea.

Marilyn had saved diligently through high school for this and even completed her senior year online so she could work full-time to save for this real estate investment. Grace and I each gave her a few thousand dollars so she could meet a twenty-five percent down payment, and then we proceeded to closing. It was early in 2007.

Little could we have known what that would mean. The closing was set to happen, but the underlying problem was that it would close only a few months after many recent scams in the real estate industry. Some of the scams were in banking; some of them were in title companies.

The loan was one of the first to close after the new lending rules and laws had been passed, and, it seemed, no one knew how to deal with the new rules. Marilyn was closing one of the first transactions in town to close under the new rules. Neither the credit union making the loan nor the closing agent, a multi-state title company, really knew how to handle the closing.

Grace and I had closed on several properties by this time in our life. I would review the documents, Grace would review the numbers, and then we would double-check each other. Title companies make many mistakes, and we've been quite fortunate to have identified most of the errors before closing. The errors we have missed have caused us significant heartaches, and title companies do their best not to stand behind their work. In all the cases, Grace and I had to pick up the pieces and cure the errors that the title companies had made. We've got stories.

At any rate, Marilyn's closing took over three and a half hours. By the end, everyone was exhausted, the credit union staff, the title company staff, Grace, me, and especially Marilyn.

The group of people sending paperwork back and forth had fixed all but one error, and, thankfully, it was a minor enough error that we all decided to let it go. We always thought purchasing a new property was a "happy thing," so Grace and I hadn't ever gone out to dinner afterward, seen a movie afterward, played a round of miniature golf afterward—only one "happy thing" at a time. That was the rule, "one happy thing at a time." Why water down the joy by adding another "something"? Another step toward our goal.

Well, this particular closing was so very difficult that we took Marilyn out to dinner. She had survived the closing. Job done.

A Place in the Washington Desert

About this time, Sam approached Grace and me and told us that the family had always wanted a place in the Washington desert and that he was ready to finance much of such a purchase. The central Washington desert is somewhat accessible from the northern valley area and is a nice place to get out of the winter rains. We had a place in Palm Springs, but we could only use that for a week or two every once in a while. Grace still had her day job.

After getting some agreement from the girls, Grace and I started looking. After many weekend trips to Leavenworth, we had decided that the property there was, even in the recession, too overpriced for our comfort zone. While on the way home from what would be our last day searching in Leavenworth, we were talking as we approached what seemed to me to be a familiar intersection. I said to Grace, "I think there is a development just down the road. Why don't I take a right turn so we can glance at properties there?"

We took that turn and started looking at condos in the development. We eventually purchased part of a nice four-plex. It was close to a swimming pool and near some really nice hiking trails. We were excited.

We enjoyed the condo for quite some time, but after a few years of owning it with little personal use and limited ability to rent it out, we sold it. We made a bit of a profit overall but definitely not enough to account for the time and effort involved. Nevertheless, it was an interesting experiment. Unfortunately, some properties just don't work.

Building 5

Recession or no recession, leases do run out, and people need to move. Some even want to own a part of the pie, part of the building where they lease. That being said, one day, out of the blue came Northwestern Men's Clinic (NWMC), and they wanted an entire floor in our Phase-4 building.

I had been working on leasing space in the "coming soon" building but hadn't had any takers. People tend to hunker down in a slow economy. Most like to see the building. E4U could not even think of paying to have a building constructed and waiting. If we were going to construct the building, we would need enough leased space to qualify for permanent financing. *Build it, and they would come?* Not in the economy we were living in.

At one point, I had even entertained the idea of leasing the to-be-constructed building to a church. The lease I drew up to my way of calculating would have been a fantastic deal for the church and would have taken me out of the straw-spreading business. Alas, thank goodness, the church's governing committee decided to look elsewhere.

NWMC was brought to us by a real estate agent, Marc McFadden. Marc understood our concept and was reasonable to deal with throughout the process. He facilitated the lease negotiations and the entry of NWMC into membership in the Phase-4 building. In my opinion, Marc McFarland personifies the type of real estate agent that really works at making a deal that is good for all parties—the seller, the buyer, and the real estate agent. He is, I believe, a real professional. Mel Clougher represented NWMC, as his son was an MD and part-owner of NWMC. Because NWMC had multiple owners, Mel had some unusual issues with our lease. He wanted all of the NWMC owners to have flexibility. We were able to work out the details, and the lease was signed.

Once the lease was signed, I went to Chris Brinkley, who facilitated construction financing through his team. In order to make the numbers work for financing, the pro forma for the building included the developer fee, the architectural fee, half the real estate leasing fee no one would have to pay, and the paid value of the lot as "paid." For financing purposes, all we asked to have financed were brick and mortar and the possible tenant improvement allowances we may need to pay in the future. The loan was very small, but we wanted it that way, so the building and E4U had the ability to carry all the stipulated costs. NWMC was paying enough rent to cover the loan costs and part of the property costs.

When we had the construction financing in place, Weller Trip assigned Darryl George as the superintendent for the building. Darryl and I had worked well throughout the construction of the Olympia building, and we pretty much knew that this building would come together well, barring unforeseen obstacles. That said, we were waiting on the permit.

Permitting for the building was not going to be as easy as keeping the permit for Building 4. We needed to go through the entire permitting process for a new building. David Weston wasn't available to work the permit through the County, so I went with Dennis Batter to do the job. Dennis is primarily a residential architect, but I needed his personality to work with the folks at the County. With Weller Trip's input, Dennis modified David's plan a little, *very little,* and added some additional space in the building. He then went to the County.

To our surprise, the building permit for Building 5 came very quickly. Now, a few years removed, that makes sense. The economy was bad. There weren't many contractors applying for permits or many buildings under construction. So it makes sense that the County employees weren't backed up with too much work. They could take time to focus, and they did. I felt we were very fortunate.

Phase 4 Building 5 Continued

That year when I went in for my annual eye exam, I found out that the optometrist was considering moving. Dr. Stanzick and I went back many years. He was the optometrist Grace had found for the family when our kids were fairly young, well before Sam was in high school. Dr. Stanzick and his wife,

Maryla, eventually signed a lease for almost half of the first floor of the to-be-constructed building. They did not want to be owners, but it was another lease. We would soon be in a position to qualify for permanent financing.

There was a bit of a glitch, however; I needed to come up with funds for Dr. Stanzick's tenant improvement funds. The only way I could figure out how to get those funds was by not paying Weller Trip for a couple of months' work. It didn't enter my mind that there would be a problem there. We had permanent financing lined up. We would just slow down payments throughout the remaining 120 days of construction, get to the permanent financing and then pay off Weller Trip.

I had been 60-days late on payments a couple of times as I scrambled for money. This delay would just be a little bit longer; I learned many years later that Ken Trip and Darryl George, both of whom were well aware that I was in a cash crunch, had a couple of significant discussions at various times during the construction of the building about if they should or should not continue construction of the building.

As I understand it, Darryl pointed out to Ken the fact that I had made all the payments on Building 4 and all the payments on Olympia. Furthermore, Darryl told me that he pointed out to Ken that he should look at my car and that it, an old, old car, proved that I wasn't a high-flying developer but just a down-to-earth person who was getting things done and paid his bills.

A short time later, probably almost four weeks, which didn't seem like a short time then, Chris Brinkley visited the construction site, determined that we had met some level of construction beyond what he expected, and he released more funds than I or Weller Trip had expected. So, between what Grace and I had saved personally and could loan to the building and what the bank was able to give us, we were able to get Weller Trip up to date. Another lucky break, and then, shortly after, the building was completed. After that, we paid off the construction loan with permanent financing, and we now had reserves at the bank for future tenant improvements.

The Campus: All Buildings Completed

And with that, the project was all completed. We still had vacancies, but all the buildings were self-supporting.

Ken Winkle, who had his own dental lab, came along and signed a lease in the Phase-4 building. Then others trickled in, but the real development was finished. Now we would need to focus on maintenance.

I was exhausted, so it was time to stop doing development work. Over the next couple of years, a few doctors approached me to take on other projects, but I just didn't have the energy or interest in doing more development. E4U had run its course.

CHAPTER 25

Final Words

Based on the numbers as we learned them while going through the process, it seems to me that we saved the buildings, their tenants, and investor members quite a bit of money using the E4U formula.

Lou Cotton and his spouse, Ann, literally saved the project with cash infusions twice, if not more often. They will, in short order, come out ahead, and the future looks pretty bright for them. Lou, Ann, Grace, and I are all still quite involved in the Cotton-Gibson Building and the other E4U buildings. We have remained good friends and strong business partners throughout this venture. Quite a team!

Darryl Houck, who left E4U early and left his $2,500 in the project, left E4U and didn't participate during the construction, so he did not get any equity in the project. Darryl and I have stayed good friends and see each other at least every couple of years. I value his friendship more and more each year. And, almost every time we get together, we ask Jimmy East to join us.

Mark Jersey, the general contractor who liked how the Cotton-Gibson building came together and drove for establishing the

E4U concept, saved the LLCs about $500,000 by contributing half his usual fee. He sold his share of the Jersey building early on but was, I heard later, upset with how much he had to pay in income taxes because of the sale. He still owns quite a large portion of Phase 2, so he or his family should receive some terrific cash payments starting sometime in the next several years when the building is paid off. Mark and I don't talk often, but he has periodically stepped up in recent years and has helped the new campus manager, Shirley, with history, recommendations, and contacts to help with various maintenance projects.

Based on my estimation, David Weston, the creator and architect of the project, saved the LLCs between $600,000 and $800,000 based on the fees he didn't charge. I feel that in the short-term, he gained the least on the project; then, as expected, he lost half of his equity in his divorce. He or his daughters should come out ahead in time. For the last several years, David and I now try to have lunch once a quarter. David continues to thrive. Recently, he remarried and took on a second home in Arizona, I believe.

Chris Brinkley has moved from the bank to a better long-term opportunity. He is now a senior executive in a company that develops large residential multifamily properties. He will do great things.

By making their own tenant improvements, the tenant owners/members not only helped with the down payment for each building but also saved the entities around a million dollars in total. Some have sold their portion of one or another of the buildings, but even those that have, haven't lost money on their E4U investment. The tenants who have kept membership in the various LLCs will be making real money soon, but in the meantime, they are improving their equity position each and every month.

By not paying real estate commissions to any but one real estate agent on the leased space, it appears that Grace and I saved the LLCs about $1.8 million.

Many people bought into the E4U concept and made the project happen. Of course, as previously mentioned, MIRATT and their money was our first gigantic break and made everything that followed. The MIRATT members have all retired and are "looking good" each time we see them at an annual LLC meeting.

Bill Hayburner died; I am saddened by his passing. However, his family has stayed invested in the building, as have the two other investors Bill brought into the investment.

As for Grace and me, we just kept the project going. By the end of the project, which took 12 years, we had not only dedicated much of 12 years of our lives to the project, but we loaned the project the equivalent of what had been more than our net worth when we started the project. We loaned the project over a million dollars. We are now getting paid back by the buildings. Eventually, we, or our kids, will benefit from the labor and equity membership we have in the campus. It will be a while, but it will have been worth it.

The Cotton-Gibson building, the Phase-1 building, and the Olympia building are already paid off and sending members cash each month. The Phase-2 building should be paid off in 4–6 years, and thanks to Shirley's hard work, it is leased until after I am gone. *Fantastic!*

Oh yes, Shirley is now managing all the commercial buildings while Grace still pays all the bills and also manages "the little properties." According to reports at the last couple of annual meetings, Shirley is doing a much better job managing the properties than I ever did. So nice to hear!

All in all, the project has been a great ride for a lot of very nice, dedicated people. We were so fortunate to be associated with so many quality people who stuck with us. I am so very glad we had the dream. We didn't want to be poor and had some very good teams and teammates.

What Now?

Let me tell you what is happening now, July 2022:

I turned 75 in April.

Grace asked me to leave shortly after our 40th anniversary in 2010. It was time. She is still my primary business partner and still keeps the books on all our joint properties. I think we both still have a lot of respect for each other. She has retired and is at home. I still wanted to do things. I think I was just difficult to be around, maybe worse.

She is a wealthy, good-looking woman and a very nice person; she spends her summers in the Seattle area and winters in Palm Desert, California.

I moved to a 55-and-older community in Vancouver, WA. At 70, I decided I would purchase a business a year until I hit 80.

I was doing well. I made many good friends. I was eating well and had learned how to cook a little. I had an extremely enjoyable situation. However, I didn't have the close contact that I like. So, I went online and started dating. Luck is so important in life. Early in my search, I met a woman named Bette. What a find. At any rate, I dated thirty or so more women to make sure I wasn't just rebound-crazy. Eventually, I made my way back to Bette. Bette and I have now been together for almost eleven years. She is funnier than funny. We have good times.

Then the first business I purchased was an HVAC company. The short story: a young kid had been calling me once a quarter for almost five years to get the contract to take care of the rooftop units on our commercial buildings. One day, the guy who has been taking care of the rooftop units for twenty years tells me he is retiring soon. The next time the young kid called me, we met. I agreed to give him access to the rooftop units and the available information I had for him to do that work. I then asked him what he wanted to do with his life.

He told me he had been the top salesperson in the Seattle area for three of the last four years.

I said, "That is great. So, is that what you are going to do for the rest of your life?"

He said, "No, what I'd really like is to own my own HVAC company."

"What's stopping you?"

"No one has any money."

Later, he now had $100,000, so we went out and bought ourselves a company. David has done a wonderful job with the company. He's taken it from $400,000 per year, and he should hit at least $3.5 million this year.

Next was a small newspaper. I worked on the paper for three years. March of 2020 was looking like its first profitable month. Between the ensuing COVID pandemic and my being diagnosed with lung cancer, the paper died. I have stage-4 lung cancer and an ALK mutation. I went from curable to 6 months to live, then slowly gained back time. I have never smoked. I have "gone vegan," as doing it is supposed to slow cancer growth. The outlook is bright. I'm hopeful.

Into the Future

Next was a 33.3 percent interest in a website: weightlossjournal. net. It is growing in the capable hands of a young person, Elias, from Austria who is currently living in Spain. I hope to meet him as soon as COVID lifts so I can travel. If we are able to put it together, you may hear some ads about the 1st

International Weight Loss Convention. I'm already working on the groundwork for 2025.

Then last year, I started with Vpfranches.com, legally known as Vantage Point Franchises and More LLC. I work with a wide variety of people, helping them transition from retirement, their day job, or their search for a franchise. A franchise gives them a road map and the ability to control their own future. Some choices are: to make more money, to build an estate for their family, to have more time with their family, to have more control of their life, and often, to get off the road. I represent over 330 franchises. Everyone is different, with a different background and different goals.

Last year, I purchased an ad, "arbitrage website." The website is hollywoodrecorder.com. As I understand it, we purchase and resell ads. It is managed out of Washington, DC. The manager gets 25 percent of the net profit. I am not sure internet advertising is the future. We shall see how this one works out.

This year I am working with a person in India who is designing a website for us to sell products on eBay, Amazon, and Spotify. Once it is up and running, he will manage it and get 50 percent of the net profit for his efforts. I found him while looking for some help. He had references that led me to believe he had tremendous potential. This morning, I received notice from eBay that they have issued a check for us. It appears "things are happening."

This evening, I will be meeting with a motivated neighbor. I've proposed to purchase a company if she will run it and split the profits with me. We shall see the outcome. Exciting times. So much opportunity. I am optimistic.

You are up to date.

Thanks for reading my book,

Gib

ACKNOWLEDGEMENTS

Getting a book published really is quite an undertaking.

I want to thank my kids: Shirley, Sam and Marilyn for encouraging me to write this book. They wanted to know 'how it happened' and kept pressing for the details.

Grace. Thank you for sticking with me and making these dreams and stories happen. You are terrific!

I thank Self-Publishing School for helping me focus and to 'get the job finished'. I especially want to acknowledge: Michael, Scott, Matt, Sean and Jordyn. Thank you all for keeping me moving toward the finish line.

> Should you want an inspirational story, look at Chandler Bolt's LinkedIn page. He and his story are both quite inspirational.

Jeannie Culbertson made this book what it is. She is the person who cleaned up what I had written and made sense of it. Thank you Noteworthy Mom.

And, I must give a lot of credit to my life partner Bette for dealing with me while I went almost completely 'off-line' for eight weeks to finish this up. Thank you, Bette.

And finally, thank you readers. Thank you for taking a chance with a first time writer. Should you have time, please write an honest review of the book at Amazon.com Thank you.

Thank You for Reading

Learn Apply & Grow Rich

If you enjoyed this book and believe it will benefit others, please take a moment to write an honest review on Amazon. Your input is valuable and genuinely appreciated.

Thank you!

Let's Connect!

Write me at continueforward@live.com for your Thank You gift.

You can find additional tools and assistance on your journey by going to my website at https://www.vpfranchises.com/. Don't forget to download your free insert freebie/lead magnet here!

Gib